Sea Otters

Sea Otters

John A. Love

With illustrations by the author

Fulcrum Publishing
Golden, Colorado

599.74
Lov

Copyright © 1992 John Love
Originally published in the United Kingdom as *Sea Otters*
Whittet Books, London
U.K. copyright © 1990 by John A. Love

Cover photo by Kennan Ward
Copyright © 1992 Kennan Ward

Cover design by Susan Hunt

Library of Congress Cataloging-in-Publication Data

Love, John A.
      Sea otters / John A. Love ; with illustrations by the author.
           p. cm.
      Includes bibliographical references and index.
      ISBN 1-55591-123-4 (pbk.)
      1. Sea otter. I. Title.
    QL737.C25L68 1992
    599.74'447–dc20

                               92-53032
                                CIP

Printed in the United States of America

0 9 8 7 6 5 4 3 2

Fulcrum Publishing
350 Indiana Street, Suite 350
Golden, Colorado 80401-5093

For Brenda

Contents

Introduction

The Old Man of the Sea

Sea otters *(Enhydra lutris)* are the largest of the world's otter species, about the size of a plump, short-legged collie dog, but quite distinct from the otter *(Lutra lutra)* that inhabits Europe and may also live in the sea. Sea otters are dark, smoky brown in color, with a pale yellowish-brown head and neck. In older animals the head looks gray and, with its prominent whiskered face, the creature assumes the appearance of a grizzled old grandfather. For this reason the sea otter is sometimes referred to as "the old man of the sea."

Sea otters are remarkable creatures. They can live out their entire lives without ever coming to land. They even give birth in the water. They rely not upon blubber but upon their dense fur to provide body warmth and insulation. To maintain the vital integrity of the fur, they have to groom constantly. At the surface the animals spend most of their time lying on their backs, often sticking one or both feet out of the water, which helps regulate body temperature. The skin surface of the large splayed feet is useful in dissipating heat if the animal is too warm, or absorbing heat from the sun if the animal is too cold. As it dozes, a sea otter may wrap strands of kelp or other seaweed around its body to keep from drifting away. Offshore kelp beds (appropriately named!) are favored haunts of resting and feeding sea otters.

The thick pelt of the sea otter proved its undoing. During the latter half of the eighteenth century and continuing into the nineteenth, sea otters were hunted to the verge of extinction because of their exquisite fur—a commodity that the Russians came to refer to as "soft gold." So valuable did the fur become to man that it accelerated the exploration and development of the North Pacific, the Bering Straits in particular. Famous pioneers such as Georg Steller (naturalist with Vitus Bering) and Captain James Cook were the first Europeans to bring otter skins back to civilization for the delectation of the wealthy. But it was the Russians who first exploited the species, enslaving the native Aleuts to hunt the otters for them. Both the Aleut and his "brother" the sea otter suffered together, the numbers of each being decimated simultaneously. For this reason the Russians colonized Alaska and even set up a base as far south as California. When the sea otters became scarce, attention turned to fur seals, whose pelts were worth only a fraction of those of the sea otters but whose population could still be numbered in millions. Only after sea otters and fur seals became so scarce as to be hardly worth pursuing did the Russians eventually pull out and in 1867 sell Alaska to the United States. Sea otters also played a part, albeit indirectly, in the American acquisition of the state of California from Mexico twenty years earlier.

This century, following a relaxation of hunting pressure and the introduction of legal protection, the remaining sea otter populations increased in numbers again. Though they have now spread to occupy much of their former habitat, much of the coastline of North America remains untenanted. Experimental reintroductions of sea otters to some localities have recently met with some success.

Although they will catch and eat fish, sea otters feed primarily upon invertebrates, especially shellfish and sea urchins. In this respect they exhibit yet another remarkable trait. Sea otters are the only mammals, other than the primates, that readily employ tools in the pursuit of food. Underwater, they use large stones to pound and dislodge shellfish prey. Particularly handy stones can be tucked under a loose fold of skin (always the left armpit) to be employed again and again. A smaller, flattish stone can also serve as an anvil. On the sea surface, otters will lie on their backs, place a stone on their chests and smash a mollusk against it. It is now known that sea otters possess an extra bone in their wrist that facilitates their shell-smashing ability. Recently these resourceful creatures have also learned to collect empty beer cans from the seabed and rip them open at the surface with their powerful teeth to get at tasty little octopuses which shelter inside.

To maintain a comfortable body temperature, sea otters have voracious appetites. They can modify offshore habitats to a considerable degree. By preying selectively upon herbivorous sea urchins, they can transform a barren seabed consisting of little other than coralline seaweeds into dense forests of kelp. This alga is a valuable resource in itself, and the fish that shelter within it can attract seals, bald eagles and even man. But *urchin barrens* (areas denuded of weed by the grazing of urchins) can be commercially important too. Just beneath the mud and silt may lie rich beds of clams and other shellfish. These are a favorite food of both man and otter, bringing the two into headlong conflict. Some illegal shooting of otters takes place, but humans also affect these unique mammals indirectly. Otters may become entangled in fishnets and drown. They are also vulnerable to pollution, especially oil spills. No one really appreciated how catastrophic such spills could be until the tanker *Exxon Valdez* ran aground on Good Friday, 1989. It is estimated that several thousand sea otters and many thousands of other marine animals may have died lingering deaths in Prince William Sound, Alaska.

Having tenaciously withstood wholesale slaughter over the last century, the sea otters are still at the mercy of man's clumsy hands. This book attempts to outline the way of life and the adaptations of this unique species, its near terminal exploitation and the modern threats that it faces.

It may seem a gross impertinence that a Scottish biologist should take it upon himself to write about a rare mammal that lives on the other side of the world. My experience of sea otters is limited to a month I spent in California in 1985. Then I had the privilege to watch the fascinating sea otter at various locations along the coast of the Sunshine State and to observe it at close quarters in captivity. Such experiences have been my inspiration.

The bulk of this book derives from the work of others too numerous to mention by name. In 1947, Barabash-Nikiforov wrote an account of the sea otter in the USSR, which was translated from Russian in 1962. But most of the research is American. Karl Kenyon wrote an inspiring book entitled *The Sea Otter in the Eastern Pacific Ocean,* which remains the fullest account of the species to date. Many other scientists have since undertaken major studies, notably Jim Estes, Glen VanBlaricom, Ron Jameson and Judson Vandevere. I am deeply indebted to them and their numerous colleagues. (Grateful thanks also to Paul Chanin, who read and commented on an earlier draft of this book, to Annabel Whittet for much editorial help and much patience and to Don and Kay Winner, who showed me my first wild sea otters.) These have been my sources and helpful contacts.

A selected list of major papers on sea otters is included at the end of this book. Indeed, the sea otter now enjoys the distinction of being one of the best studied mammals in the world. But much of this material lies buried in books, reports and learned journals, few of which are readily available even in North America. The definitive monograph on the species remains to be written. This book does not attempt that truly daunting task but strives only to bring together something of what is known in an easily readable and readily accessible volume. Furthermore, it is directed principally at a readership who have remained in ignorance of this endearing "seagoing teddy bear"—a situation much to be lamented. This then has been my justification for writing the book, and my motive.

Here, now, is the result.

John Love
March 1990

1

The Evolution of Sea Otters

Four-fifths of this planet is ocean. In a curious quirk of semantics, our so-called "green" earth actually looks blue from outer space. So it is not surprising that in this primordial salty soup life should have had its beginnings, over 3,000 million years ago. Many eons passed before animals and plants ventured onto dry land. A mere (geologically speaking) 350 million years ago, fish made the first bold steps, eventually evolving into newts, salamanders, frogs and toads, four thousand species of which still survive and are collectively classed as amphibians. Although able to walk about quite freely on land and breathe air, amphibians have a skin that is permeable to water. Thus, they must return to the water at intervals to soak themselves and to lay their eggs. Only when a strategy to obviate this necessity for water evolved did the reptiles develop. Some of the sixty-five hundred species of reptiles that still share this planet with us have been so successful in shrugging off a dependence upon water that they thrive in the hottest deserts. Other reptiles chose to return to the sea. The fishlike ichthyosaurs and the long-necked plesiosaurs are now extinct. Crocodiles (direct descendants of the dinosaurs), sea turtles, terrapins and sea snakes are the only aquatic survivors of a diverse group that dominated the earth 200 million years ago. Paradoxically, it is to dry land that they must come to lay their eggs, a complete reversal of the reproductive habits of their ancestral amphibians.

Seventy million years ago, while the mighty dinosaurs still stalked the earth, tiny unobtrusive mammallike creatures scuttled in the undergrowth beneath their feet. They were warmblooded, hairy and gave birth to live young that were nurtured on their mother's milk. These were the mammals of the future, eventually to inherit the earth. Flying reptiles—which we call birds—came to rule the air. Scientists have long argued about how the dinosaurs came to abdicate their terrestrial domain in the first place. It seems that a huge meteorite could have been involved. When it hit the earth—a catastrophe in itself—the shock waves probably triggered a violent series of volcanic eruptions. The dense smoke and debris clouds virtually changed the earth's climate overnight. The huge, slow-maturing dinosaurs could not adapt to the rapid changes in their habitat and soon died out.

Fur seal

So when the dust finally settled, the early mammals found themselves freed from the bonds of reptilian competition. They flourished and diversified, although only four thousand or so species still inhabit the planet today. Some eat insects, many eat plants or fruit, some even eat other animals. Most are terrestrial—although bats have developed the power of flight and, being mostly nocturnal, they have largely avoided competition with birds. But at intervals throughout their evolutionary history, mammals have been drawn back to the water's edge to devise new ways of exploiting this vast resource, which was so long the preserve of fish and a bewildering host of invertebrate animals.

One of the earliest whalelike fossils was renamed *Zeuglodon*. It had the streamlined and torpedo-shaped body typical of whales, with tail flukes to provide forward propulsion. Its front limbs looked and functioned like paddles, while its hind limbs were very much reduced. From such a beginning, about 50 million years ago, evolved the seventy present-day species of whales and dolphins collectively known as cetaceans. They are completely aquatic, even giving birth and suckling their single calf in the water. The only concession to their terrestrial ancestry is having to return to the ocean's surface at regular intervals to snatch breaths of air.

Ten million years later mammals again experimented in the sea, though fewer species were in this group. Its four surviving representatives are called sea cows or sirenians. A fifth species, Steller's sea cow (now extinct), was named after its discoverer Georg Steller, a naturalist on Vitus Bering's Arctic expedition and a prominent figure in the story of the sea otter. The other four species of sea cow—manatees and dugongs—are restricted to warmer coastal rivers and shallows where, true to their herbivorous ancestry, they graze unobtrusively on sea grasses and algae. In appearance and habits they are somewhat reminiscent of portly, sluggish whales. It is thought that these inelegant creatures, with their lumpish yet kindly countenances, gave rise to the legend of mermaids—surely the warped consequence of early mariners spending months or even years at sea.

A GOLIATH IN THE KELP BEDS

When Vitus Bering and his crew were shipwrecked on the Commander Islands in the Bering Straits, they had to spend a miserable winter eating whatever they could gather. Fortunately for them there was no shortage of seabirds, seals and sea otters. They also killed a species of sea cow whose flesh Georg Steller considered to be as good as veal. These sea cows foraged in large family parties among the offshore kelp beds, often with hungry gulls perched unconcernedly on their backs. Steller found he could even stroke the gentle giants. "Signs of a wonderful intelligence I could not observe," wrote the naturalist, "but they displayed such an uncommon love for one another that, when one of them was hooked, all the rest became intent upon saving him." Weighing as much as 9,000 pounds (over 4,000 kg) and almost 26 feet (8 m) in length, each sea cow fed fifty men for two weeks—a handsome feast for the famished crewmen.

Steller's sea cow (even when mature) was toothless and possessed short, coarse hairs on its flippers. The naturalist dissected a large female and preserved its hide. Unfortunately, the following summer when the men finally built a small boat to take them to safety, Steller had to leave nearly all his biological specimens—and, of course, a giant sea cow skin

The Evolution of Sea Otters **5**

stuffed with straw came at rock bottom of the proposed passenger list! No other scientist was ever to set eyes on Steller's sea cow again.

Being so docile, the species was especially easy meat for the sea-otter hunters who returned to the Commanders in search of the fabulous skins that Bering's crew had introduced to the world. In the wintertime, the sea cows became so thin that their ribs and spine protruded through their rough, barklike skin—this at a time of year when a thick layer of blubber was vital to insulate a marine mammal from the cold. Where once the sea cow may have ranged across the North Pacific coast from Japan to California, by 1741 it seems to have been restricted to the icy waters around the Commander Islands. Within thirty years Steller's sea cow was extinct.

Steller's sea cow

Twenty million years ago, mammals tested the water once again. These mammals were carnivorous—not herbivorous—and evolved into the familiar seals and sea lions of today. Pinnipeds, as they are known, still adhere to the torpedo-shaped body with paddlelike forelimbs and employ thick blubber as insulation against the cold. But, unlike whales and sea cows, they have retained the furry or hairy coat so characteristic of land mammals; they also have modified rear limbs, rather than tail flukes, to provide propulsion. Sea lions can even point their hind flippers forward, giving them more mobility on land than true seals, which lurch forward awkwardly on their bellies. It was essential that the pinnipeds retain at least some ability to move on land, for they must return to shore to give birth.

Nearly all of Earth's mammals can swim if they must. Most mammal groups have their amphibious representative or representatives. Having developed the habit only comparatively re-

6 Sea Otters

Yapok, or marsupial water opossum

cently, these animals have diverged much less from the ancestral four-footed blueprint than have the so-called marine mammals. The duck-billed platypus of Australia and the South American yapok (or marsupial water opossum) must be the most senior of these amphibious citizens. Among later placental mammals we have a variety of other amphibians: the insectivorous water shrew and otter shrew, the desman and tenrec. Rodents are well represented by the capybara, beaver, coypu, muskrat, water vole and fish-eating rats. Ungulates, or hoofed mammals, strive to qualify with various swamp deer and antelopes such as waterbuck—with the ungainly hippo perhaps the best qualified. All these creatures, from water shrew to waterbuck (excepting the hippo), rely on a dense, oily fur as a waterproof coat and have webbed, hairy or splayed feet or else a flattened tail to aid in swimming. One would expect the marsupial yapok to encounter special problems underwater, but its brood pouch with its precious cargo of youngsters can be tightly closed by sphincter muscles and made watertight with an oily secretion on the fur.

We have yet to mention swimming representatives among the true carnivores. Unlike most other cats, the jaguar of South America is not averse to entering the water, while the southeast Asian fishing cat regularly does so to catch its piscine prey. So do

The Evolution of Sea Otters 7

Otter shrew (left) and European water shrew

otter civets from the same area, the rare aquatic genet from Zaire and the African marsh mongoose. The riverine habitat of the mink has necessitated a fur that is much sought-after in the fashion trade. Another carnivore, the raccoon, derives its name from a Native North American word meaning "he who scratches with his hands." This refers to the animal's habit of washing its prey before eating. The crab-eating raccoon is the most aquatic of the group—although it does not eat crabs! The crab-eating fox does, however. Most of the omnivorous bears enjoy a good swim, but the polar bear can be considered the most amphibious, if only because some individuals may live out their entire lives on the sea ice without ever setting foot on terra firma. They are well adapted to catching the bulk of their food from the cold waters of the Arctic and are the most carnivorous of the bears, eating seals and fish.

There is one final group of carnivorous mammals that we all associate with water—the otters. It is difficult to be precise as to how many species we are talking about, since scientists have yet to agree on a definitive classification. One book by C. J. Harris lists no fewer than nineteen species (and sixty-three subspecies). A more recent study has reduced the total to thirteen species in four genera, namely:

Lutra— eight species including our own river otter,
Pteronura—   the giant otter of South America,

8   Sea Otters

Aonyx— two African clawless otters and the Asian small-clawed otter,
Enhydra— the sea otter of the North Pacific.

However, current opinion seems to favor two further genera, removing two species of *Lutra* otters into genera of their own—the African spotted-necked otter to *Hydrictis* and the Indian smooth-coated otter to *Lutrogale*. The remaining assortment of Lutra subspecies are lumped together into only three species— the Eurasian and American river otters and the marine otter of South America.

The earliest recognizably aquatic otter in the fossil record lived 30 million years ago. Although the group has been distinct for so long, they have remained unmistakably weasel in shape and form. All otters belong to the group of *Carnivora* called *Mustelidae*. Sea otters are the largest of the family. Early in otter evolution these unusual animals went their own way, diverging into two distinct groups. One led to the extinct genus *Enhydriodon*—three species from Eurasia and Africa that were as large if not larger than our modern sea otter. It is not known whether they were marine or freshwater in habit. The second line led to two species of *Enhydritherium*, one known from fossil deposits in Spain and the other from deposits in Florida and California; both apparently lived in the sea. About 2 million years ago one population was to become isolated in the North Pacific, where it gave rise to the genus *Enhydra*. A larger species, *Enhydra macrodonta*, is now extinct, while the other is *Enhydra lutris*—our modern sea otter.

Although this is now its accepted official title, when first discovered the sea otter was classified under the Latin name *Lutra marina*. In 1758, the Swedish taxonomist Carl Linnaeus called it *Mustela lutris*, but soon afterward it came to wallow in a veritable confusion of Latin nomenclature, finally becoming accepted as *Enhydra lutris* in 1922. While *lutris* is the Latin for "otter," *en hydra* is in fact Greek, meaning "in the water."

Many otters are equally at home on land and can run as fast as a man for short distances with a bounding, hump-backed gait. But it is in the water that they come into their own. Most or all of their food is sought in the water. Otters are efficient swimmers due

The Evolution of Sea Otters **9**

Polar bear

to their webbed feet and lithe, sinuous bodies, which are covered in dense, waterproof fur. Stiff whiskers on their snouts are sensitive to water turbulence and aid in the search for prey. However many species one chooses to recognize, all otters forage in one of two ways. *Lutra* otters and the giant otter catch fish, which they capture in their jaws. For this they have typically carnivorous teeth for shearing and cutting up flesh. The remaining species feed mainly on invertebrates, rummaging in mud and stones to find crabs, crayfish or shellfish. Two *Aonyx* species have only partially webbed forefeet, but their fingers and flexible thumb are particularly adept at handling food. Indeed, in German they are known as "finger otters." Their teeth are suited for a shearing function, while the sea otters' teeth are flattened for crushing.

The short-clawed otter is the smallest of the group, measuring 24 to 40 inches (60 to 100 cm) from head to tail and weighing about 11 pounds (5 kg). At the other extreme is the aptly named giant otter, 79 inches (200 cm) long and weighing 66 pounds (30 kg). Although not quite so long, sea otters can actually tip the scales at 100 pounds (45 kg). They may be found loafing together offshore in large, single-sex rafts but tend to feed within small individual territories. On the other hand, small-clawed, smooth-coated and giant otters live in extended family groups and clawless otters remain together in pairs. *Lutra* species tend to lead solitary lives, pairing up only in the breeding season.

THE GIANT OTTER

Twenty years after Georg Steller published his long and important account of the sea otter, the Swedish taxonomist Carl Linnaeus opted to consider it merely a northern form of the giant otter, first described in 1648. While the two species are indeed similar in size, the latter is a paler, milk-chocolate color with a conspicuous whitish yellow throat patch. It was not until 1777 that the little-known giant otter from the steaming jungles of South America came to be separated from the more familiar, furbearing animal of Alaska's icy fogs. The giant otter (*Pteronura brasiliensis*) did share the unhappy prospect of being hunted for its pelt. This century, Peru alone exported some two thousand skins annually. By 1969 only forty-seven could be collected, and the following year hunting was forbidden altogether. The species was considered so endangered that in 1975 it became protected in most other South American countries too. Only in the more remote jungle rivers of Surinam and Guyana, where hunting had ceased two decades earlier, did the giant otter remain in any significant numbers.

Sharing its range with a subspecies of the river otter, the elusive giant is more diurnal in habits than its cousin. Family groups of three to eight (sometimes as many as

Giant otters

The Evolution of Sea Otters **11**

twenty) defend a territory, which they stake out with communal riverside latrines. These so-called campsites are cleared of vegetation so that the residents can trample in their smelly feces and urine to warn off intruding otters. The cubs, usually one to three in number, are born in underground lairs nearby. Although the previous year's young may still be around, they do not seem to participate in rearing the new litter. They do prove useful in hunting, on the premise that a group of otters "otter be" more successful than lone individuals! While not exactly deliberately cooperating, several foraging otters probably disturb and confuse the fish, making them easier to catch.

Except in the case of sea otters, all otter cubs are born in isolated lairs, often underground. According to species, litter size can be as many as five or six cubs but is more usually two or three; the sea otter has only one cub (twins are exceedingly rare). Otter cubs are reared by the female only, although in *Aonyx* species the male also plays his part.

Most otters frequent rivers, streams, marshes, sometimes coastal swamps. The small and rare marine otter, sea cat or chungungo (*Lutra felina*) inhabits the wild rocky coasts of Chile and Peru, formerly as far south as Cape Horn. It is less well adapted to a marine existence than the sea otter. Not only does it sometimes penetrate upriver but it must come ashore to give birth (in burrows). Large prey is also brought ashore, smaller items being consumed on the water while the chungungo floats belly up just like a sea otter. At forty-five seconds, its dives are of similar duration to those of sea otters, but fish seem to be its main prey, together with some crustaceans, urchins, mollusks and various

Sea otter

12 Sea Otters

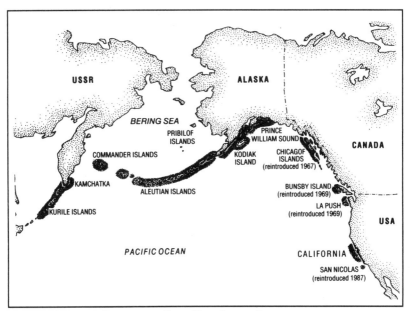

Current distribution of sea otters

marine worms. In contrast to sea otters, male and female chungungos are of similar size and are one of the smallest otter species—weighing about 11 pounds (5 kg). They were once hunted extensively by South American Indians as a food source and for the valuable fur. This little-known creature is now extinct in Argentina, and, farther north, fewer than a thousand may survive in total.

THE EUROPEAN OTTER AT SEA

To distinguish it from the sea otter, the North American subspecies of the European otter, *Lutra lutra*, is usually referred to as the river otter. In some parts of the New World river otters may frequent the sea, but this habit is more developed in otters in northern Britain and Scandinavia. As long ago as the ninth century, Saint Cuthbert is said to have

The Evolution of Sea Otters **13**

emerged from paddling in the sea one day along the Berwickshire coast to have his feet rubbed dry by two obliging otters. Nowadays, due to human disturbance, only the northern shores of mainland Scotland, the Hebrides, Orkney and Shetland are free enough from human disturbance to permit otters to thrive there. Indeed, because of habitat loss and pollution in inland lakes and rivers, a significant proportion of British otters now live on the northern shores. Just like the sea otter of the North Pacific, they prefer shelving, rocky coastlines with dense offshore beds of kelp. Bare sandy areas, where fish are scarce, tend to be avoided. But being less well adapted to a marine existence, European otters must keep their fur clean of salt to maintain its waterproof quality, so they regularly return to fresh water, be it a small rivermouth or lake, to wash or to drink.

And, of course, European otters must come ashore to give birth, their underground lairs being located in rock cairns or under peaty banks near the sea. They tend to be solitary creatures, associating in pairs for a short time only. Mating takes place either in the water or on land. In northern Britain, otter cubs are usually born in early summer, when fish are abundant. A normal litter consists of two, perhaps three, cubs, which are born covered in short, pale gray down. Unlike sea otters, the cubs' eyes do not open until the otters are about five weeks old, and the cubs do not emerge from the lair to take their first swim until they are two or three months old. In coastal situations the dives of European otters average about twenty seconds, and some 20 percent of the dives result in the capture of prey. Around 90 percent of the diet is fish, usually 6 to 8 inches (15 to 20 cm) long, with larger fish being brought to shore to be eaten. The remainder of their diet is crabs, which take longer to deal with and, being less nutritious, are eaten only if fish are hard to come by. Younger, inexperienced otters resort to crabs more often than do adults.

In northern Scotland otters have been known to drown in fishnets or crab pots, and in 1978 at least fourteen were killed by a spill of twelve hundred tons of fuel oil in the Sullom Voe Terminal in Shetland. Hunting was long the most

European otters

serious cause of mortality, with special otter hounds being employed in southern Britain, while guns and traps were used in the north. Between 1876 and 1885, for instance, over a hundred otters were killed on the islands of Lewis and Harris alone.

Now, happily, otters are protected in Britain and, in the north at least, the species is beginning to show the trust in man that it first displayed to Saint Cuthbert a thousand years ago. Otters have been known to take up residence under piers or in barns or sheds. The women's restroom at one ferry terminal in Shetland was the regular haunt of one otter—but whether it was of the sex entitled to use that facility was never determined. Another otter reared no less than nine cubs, over several breeding seasons, under a jetty at Sullom Voe, proving that oil and "otter" can mix successfully!

The sea otter originally ranged from northern Hokkaido in Japan and southern Sakhalin in Siberia through the Kurile Islands to the outer coast of Kamchatka. From there, at about 60° north, the species then extended eastward to the Commander Islands. These otters are the smallest representatives of the species and are classified as a separate subspecies, *Enhydra lutris gracilis*. Then there is a sea gap of 185 miles (298 km) to the outer Aleutian

The Evolution of Sea Otters **15**

Islands of Alaska, where the greatest population of sea otters surviving today is found. This population extends from Attu, the outermost of the Near Island group, through the long chain of the Aleutians—Amchitka (one of the Rat Islands), the Andreanofs, the Fox Islands of Unalaska, Unimak and others—to the Alaskan peninsula itself. Two hundred miles to the north lie the isolated Pribilof Islands, where sea otters once also thrived. The species extended along the southern Alaskan coast through Kodiak Island and Prince William Sound to Sitka. Farther south, along the British Columbian coast including the Queen Charlotte Islands, otters were less numerous, reaching into the states of Washington and Oregon. All these populations were grouped into a second subspecies of larger animals and named *Enhydra lutris lutris*. A third, slightly smaller subspecies, *Enhydra lutris nereis*, populated the Californian coast and offshore islands as far south as Morro Hermoso (27° 32' N) in Baja California, Mexico.

Along this huge crescent of North Pacific coast the species suffered persecution during the late eighteenth and nineteenth centuries that reduced it to a mere handful of remnant populations early this century. However, that is a long and tragic story; first let us investigate the fascinating adaptations that the sea otter has evolved to permit it to thrive in such a variety of climatic conditions—the most northerly of them seemingly quite inhospitable.

RETURN TO BIG SUR

On March 19, 1938, a farmer looked out from his clifftop residence near Big Sur, 13 miles south of Carmel in California, and spotted a strange group of animals riding the surf far below. Training a telescope on them, he realized they were far too small for seals and had "odd-shaped flippers that seemed to grow from their backs." He reported his observation, and someone suggested they might be sea otters. The scientists remained skeptical. "Since the southern sea otter has been considered as practically extinct, this report has been received with elevated eyebrows," wrote the *Journal of Mammalogy* that same year. "A single sea otter, or possibly a pair, might be conceivable, but their presence in large numbers seemed to be beyond belief." Apparently, one scientist later admitted, "Had you reported dinosaurs or ichthyosaurs . . . we couldn't have been more utterly dumbfounded."

The local newspapers were less restrained and soon were reporting crowds of people gathering to watch two or three hundred sea otters. The scientists eventually conceded that the discovery was "not particularly surprising when the character of the coast is taken into consideration. The region has been comparatively inaccessible and was first opened to through motor traffic during the summer of 1937. Sheer cliffs . . . rise directly from the sea . . . making access to the beach difficult. . . . They have probably been seen several times during the past two decades but remained unrecognized, since from a distance the sea otters might easily be mistaken by a casual observer for seals or sea lions." This had indeed been true; sea otters had been seen in the past, but local naturalists preferred to keep the little colony a closely guarded secret.

One of the first scientists who took time to study the sea otters was Dr. Edna Fisher of the University of California. In an important paper published in 1939, she reported a unique sequence of behavior. "It is not an uncommon thing to hear a sharp clicking sound . . . made by an otter that is trying to crack something open. . . . The object is held in both paws and, with full arm action from well over the head, it is brought down hard on a piece of rock that rests on the otter's chest."

In 1941, a sea otter refuge was declared that stretched from Malpaso Creek to just south of Big Sur. Responding to a subsequent expansion of the animals' range, the refuge was extended in 1959 from Carmel to Cambria. The use of firearms and low-flying aircraft was prohibited.

The Evolution of Sea Otters **17**

2

Anatomy of an Otter

The sea otter is the smallest of the truly marine mammals, and it is unique in many additional respects. In outward appearance it is the least modified to an aquatic existence, but, like the whales and sirenians, practically all its ties with land have been severed. Seals and sea lions must come ashore to give birth. The sea otter is able to give birth at sea, and it only comes ashore when it wants to. This option is rarely exercised by the otters that live along the coast of California.

Yet on land the sea otter can run well, albeit with a curious rolling and bounding gait, somewhat reminiscent of a lumbering sea lion. The body is relatively long and heavy for an otter, making its progress seem slower and more clumsy than it actually is. The tail is quite short, about one-third the length of the head and body. It is slightly flattened to assist in swimming, which is achieved by vertical undulations of the rear end, in a style similar to that of whales and dolphins. But instead of tail flukes, the propulsive force derives principally from the hind feet. Indeed the sea otter's pelvis and femur are suitably modified to give the hind limbs extra freedom of movement. Its ribs and sternum are also rather loosely articulated, and each vertebra has reduced bony processes (which serve as attachment for muscles but can inhibit movement somewhat). All these features make the skeleton more supple for swimming.

The back feet are decidedly flipperlike and webbed right to the tips of the long toes. The fifth or outermost digit on each foot is the longest and is closely bound to the fourth digit to give a more

Sea otter on land

Anatomy of an Otter **21**

extensive and rigid surface against the water. A final kick upward with the splayed feet gives additional acceleration at each stroke. By these means the animal can achieve comfortable speeds of up to 3 miles (5 km) per hour, doubling this if it needs to escape from a tricky situation. Separate paddling movements of the hind feet give the otter maneuverability as it swims about on the sea floor. At the surface it almost invariably lies on its back, moving about by casually sculling from side to side with its feet and tail.

SLIPPERY CUSTOMERS

Although not especially fast, sea otters are remarkably agile. Alaskan scientists were chasing one in a boat one day, and as soon as the craft came up to the animal the man in the bows plunged in his dip net. The otter's momentum took it into the mouth of the net, but quickly realizing what had happened, the creature somersaulted to reverse direction. It then darted to freedom before the man had time to snatch the net, with its prize, out of the water. Another otter was pursued by a boat for no less than 50 minutes. In that time she made thirteen dives in quick succession to avoid capture. These averaged 2 minutes and the maximum was 4.2 minutes. Her last dive of 3.5 minutes was one of the longest and indicated that the otter had plenty of strength left. The chase was finally abandoned as futile.

The small claws on the front feet are retractable, a feature not exhibited by any other otter species. The front paws are webbed, but when the animal is swimming they are rarely used, being held palm-side down or folded against the chest. They have tough leathery pads (absent in the hind feet) to facilitate grasping slippery prey. The paws are also well served with sensitive nerve endings so that the animal can feel about on the bottom for prey. Indeed, the area of brain dealing with sensory information from the forelimbs is enlarged, as are those connected with the facial area, the snout and the sixty or so stiff whiskers sprouting on each side of the black nose. One captive otter had these hairs trimmed away by its well-meaning but inquiring keeper. Until the whiskers regrew, the poor animal took four times longer to detect and catch prey in muddy water. It was unaffected in clear water, being able to rely on its sight instead. In turbid water sea otters resort to their sense of touch. When one captive was allowed to dip into a bucket of muddy water it immediately plucked out four mussels hidden among a mass of stones and small crabs. Skin divers have also watched wild otters probing rather than looking for food, feeling into nooks and crannies on the sea floor, all the while holding their heads well back.

To see better underwater, all species of otter can alter the shape of the lens in the eye, making it more spherical. Sea otter sight is not particularly good, certainly no better than that of other otters and not as good as that of seals. Several wild otters with sight only in one eye seemed healthy enough. One captive with such a disability survived for five years; during its final year it was blind in both eyes. Only one completely blind sea otter has been reported in the wild; it was very emaciated and close to death. Although the species does not normally feed at nighttime, mothers with young cubs are sometimes forced to do so and manage perfectly well. On land sea otters rely upon smell rather than sight, but their sense of hearing must also prove useful. Sea otters have small, slightly rolled ears, more like those of a sea lion than those of other mammals, even the river otter. The ears can be held erect or pointed downward when the animal is on the surface, but when diving they are closed off by muscular action to keep water from getting in.

Living so much in the sea, sea otters obviously find fresh water hard to come by. Captive otters may drink as much as two quarts a day, but nearly three-quarters of the animal's liquid requirements are normally gained from its food. The remainder is obtained by drinking sea water. A sea otter shows no particular preference even if fresh water is available. In order to excrete the additional salt load, the kidney of the sea otter is enlarged (about twice that of the river otter) and amounts to about 2 percent of its body weight. Like those of other marine mammals, the kidney is

Anatomy of an Otter **23**

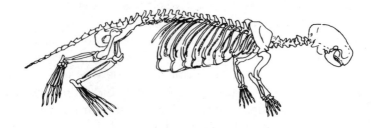

Sea otter skeleton

very lobed in structure and produces a very concentrated urine to rid the body of excess salt. River otters are sometimes found living on the sea coast, in the north of Scotland for instance. However, they remain highly dependent upon fresh water, coming ashore to streams and small lakes to bathe and, presumably, also to drink. Captive river otters denied access to fresh water become very distressed; their fur becomes soiled and soon loses its insulative properties.

Sea otters help to maintain their body warmth by having a rapid metabolism, about two and a half times that of a terrestrial mammal. To sustain this metabolic rate, the animals have a hearty appetite. Captive sea otters eat 25 to 30 percent of their body weight each day, so wild ones, being more active, will have to consume even more. To cope with this, the otter's gut is well developed; it is ten times the length of its body. As a comparison, the gut of a dog or cat, for instance, is only four times as long as the animal's body. The digestion of food in the sea otter is rapid, passing through the alimentary tract in about three hours, with a digestive efficiency estimated to be about 80 or 85 percent. In order to cope with this amount of food the liver is also exceptionally large, equaling about 6 percent of body weight and proportionately twice as heavy as that of other marine mammals. Cetaceans, seals and sea cows can store extra food as blubber, which also serves to aid buoyancy in the water and acts as vital insulation. Sea otters are lean creatures and derive buoyancy from their fur and their lungs. The latter are twice as large as expected; the rib cage and thoracic cavity are also enlarged to accommodate

24   Sea Otters

them. The lungs store two-thirds of the animal's oxygen needs while it is underwater, the remainder being stored in the muscles and blood. In common with seals, the sea otter's blood is more concentrated in hemoglobin than that of terrestrial mammals.

Like most other mammals, the sea otter has a body temperature of 100°F (38°C), but heat can be lost through the limbs, which are more sparsely covered in hair. In order to retain heat, the blood destined for the appendages is cooled down before it becomes exposed to cold water or air. This is achieved by a heat exchange system. The arteries in the limbs lie alongside the veins so that as blood enters the limbs it is cooled, the heat transferring to the colder venous blood coming in from the extremities. Thus, not too much heat is lost from the body, and the legs are able to function well at colder temperatures in any case. Heat is generated from activity, so if an animal is moving about a lot, the danger can be less one of losing heat than of overheating inside its ultra-effective thermal jacket. The sea otter seems to possess an extra network of blood vessels so that, after strenuous exercise, these bypass vessels open up to release more blood into the limbs for cooling. Thus, in water of 79°F (26°C), two-thirds of an otter's heat load can be shed through the flippers. This cooling can be increased even more by air contact, and often sea otters can be seen lying at the surface with their hind feet splayed to expose the maximum surface area for cooling. In fact, the system probably works in reverse in cold conditions, when the splayed feet can absorb heat from the sun to raise the body temperature. If an otter becomes dangerously overheated, water can be allowed to seep into the air spaces in the fur to cool the skin directly. The animal can then be seen to lie lower in the water because it has lost buoyancy. Surely this technique can only be a last-ditch method, since the otter has less control over the consequences. But by such various adjustments to control its body heat, the sea otter is able to withstand a wide range of environmental temperatures in waters from 68°F (20°C) to -4°F (-20°C).

But, of course, one adaptation of the sea otter, crucial to its survival, remains to be discussed—its fur. Paradoxically, this luxurious commodity was to become a liability, but the fur trade it attracted will be discussed in the next chapter. An otter's coat provides it with buoyancy in the water, it helps maintain body warmth and it is waterproof. As insulation, thick hair is apparently four times as effective as fat. However, compared with other terrestrial mammals of northern climes, the pelt of the sea otter is not especially remarkable for its insulative properties. What is special is its water resistance, which retains its insulative property even in icy water.

Because their fur can become easily soiled, captive otters need adequate opportunity to groom. One captive individual was observed spending nearly half of the daylight hours engaged in this essential activity. In the wild such attentions seem less necessary, taking perhaps only 5 to 11 percent of the animal's time. The treatment is undertaken in the water. The fur is rubbed meticulously with the palms of the forepaws, the animal contorting its body or rolling within its loose skin to reach the awkward parts. The hind paws are rubbed together or stroked against the flanks and abdomen. Folds of skin are then squeezed between the forepaws, or with the tongue, to remove moisture. Finally, the otter may lie on its belly in the water, bending its head underneath to blow air into the fur. Alternatively, it may aerate its fur with a rapid churning motion of the paws, which beat the water to a foaming froth. The air bubbles get trapped among the dry underfur to serve as vital insulation. The otter rolling at the surface

Sea otter grooming

26   Sea Otters

smooths and rearranges its fur neatly. A well-aerated, dry fur visibly increases the otter's buoyancy, a feature most strikingly demonstrated in a small, fluffy cub, lovingly groomed to perfection by an attentive mother.

The fur of sea otters is highly variable in color, mostly a deep, lustrous brown, brightened with silver-gray speckles. Some animals are a grayish brown, some yellowish brown, others a dark plum color and yet others almost black. The blacker a pelt and the more regularly dispersed its silver tips, the greater its commercial value. Albinos with pure white fur are rare. Steller recorded one on the Kurile Islands and another on the Commander Islands, where a third was seen in 1899. The abdomen of a normal otter tends to be a lighter color than its back, while the hairs on the head and neck are lighter still. Older individuals often become even paler and look distinctly grizzled.

Individual hairs are a smoky brown color, becoming lighter toward the base. They measure about 1 inch (23 mm) in length. Darker guard hairs, .25 to .5 inch (5 to 10 mm) longer and slightly flattened toward the base, protrude through this coat. Their function probably is to protect the underfur, giving it mechanical support so that it can trap the insulating pockets of air more effectively.

A single guard hair emanates from each follicle in the skin, together with some sixty to eighty underfur hairs. These bundles resemble those of fur seals but are more densely distributed and have twice as many hairs to each follicle. In fact, having about 700,000 hairs per square inch (108,500 per square cm), the sea otter's fur is twice as dense as that of the river otter and is the densest fur of any mammal. Someone has even gone to the trouble of calculating that the pelt of an adult sea otter may contain as many as 800 million individual hairs!

Historically, sea otters were able to be hunted throughout the year because they have no distinct season for shedding old hairs, an adaptation that the sea otter shares with its river cousin, keeping its fur thick and warm. Hairs are shed reluctantly, so an adult may eventually come to possess twice as many in each bundle as a youngster. The absence of erector muscles in the thick, oily skin, which would otherwise serve to pull the hair

Anatomy of an Otter **27**

Grooming again

bundles upright, results in the fur lying close to the skin surface when the animal submerges, which, with the flattened tips of the guard hairs, improves waterproofing.

Sea otter skin is extremely loose-fitting, as though the animal had the worst of all possible tailors. In fact, this quality enables the otter to pull its skin around to reach even the least accessible parts for grooming, an activity that is crucial to retaining the integrity of the fur. One biologist has even joked that when a sea otter is picked up, "the abdominal contents slosh to the end that is down!" When the animal is skinned, the pelt can be stretched half as long again as the body and, weighing 3.3 pounds (1.5 kg), will cover an area of over 13 square feet (1.2 square m). The larger the fur, of course, the more it is worth to the fur trade. Commercial preparation involved scraping fatty tissue from the underside of the skin. The skin was then smeared with oil or grease, the excess being removed by tumbling the entire fur in sawdust. The pelts of other furbearing mammals require the removal of the guard hairs, a process invented by the Chinese in the middle of the eighteenth century. Sea otter furs did not require this time-consuming and costly treatment, a factor that greatly enhanced their value. Poor quality furs could be upgraded by smoking. This unethical treatment temporarily changed the color from a light yellowish brown to the more sought-after dark brown, but only long enough to fetch a better price. After auction a low quality skin might then be dyed. Complete immersion in the dye solution colored the hide as well, so some crafty dealers learned to escape detection by brushing the dye directly onto the hairs — a process called "topping"—leaving the leather its natural color.

Although the value of sea otter pelts could vary according to size, color and quality, the pelts remained by far the most valuable of all commercial furs in the northwest Pacific. The relentless quest for them made a fortune for many white men, and the trade had a profound effect on the region's history and development, both political and economic. It also had a devastating effect on the region's otter populations and even upon the native Aleut peoples who were forced to hunt them.

3

The Fur Trade

Spanish missionaries in Baja California were the first Europeans to set eyes on sea otters. In 1733, Father Sigismundo Taraval visited the island of Cedros and "found such numbers of them together that the seamen killed about twenty by following them only with sticks." Some of the skins the padre sent to Mexico. Doubtless other missionaries and explorers who ventured into California at the time also bartered for otter skins with the natives.

The natives of course had been familiar with the species for thousands of years. Sea otter bones have been excavated from native rubbish dumps or middens dating back three thousand years. The pelts do not seem to have been especially important to them; in such an amiable climate men had little need to wear warm clothing. Burnt otter bones indicate that the animals might have provided an occasional meal. The Native Americans caught them by spreading nets and snares on the kelp beds offshore. One rather cruel technique seems so time-consuming it mercifully might not have been used too often. When a Native American spotted a mother and cub, he watched until she submerged, leaving the helpless baby at the surface. Paddling out to catch the cub, the Indian then attached to it numerous hooks and a long line.

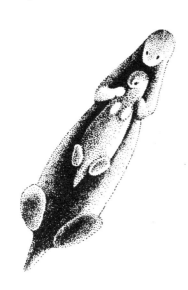

Aleut charm of a sea otter

By pulling on the line from a short distance away, the Indian could force the cub to cry out in pain. The distraught mother would immediately rush to the rescue. Preoccupied in trying to free her baby, she too become entangled and could be easily approached and clubbed to death.

But the California Indians were not as accomplished in catching sea otters as the Aleut peoples of Alaska. These tribes had diverged from other Eskimos some four thousand years before and, in the comparative isolation of the Aleutian Island chain, had evolved their own dis-

The Fur Trade 33

Unungun bronze dart head

Bone harpoon head, Fox Islands

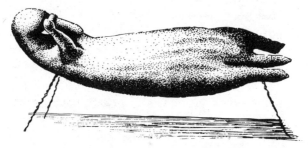

Wooden float to attach to sea otter nets

tinctive culture. The Aleuts had long shared an affinity with the sea otter—here at the northern limit of its range—whom they referred to as "our brother." They recognized in its antics much human behavior and so accorded it human origins. The Aleuts and the otter shared this harsh, unforgiving coastline, which one missionary described as "a region so gloomy, so piteously beaten by wind and waves, by sleet and rain and persistent fog that the . . . curriculum of hell [ought] to be omitted from the church breviary since these people had enough of it here on this earth!"

Like the Californian natives, the Aleuts had been hunting sea otters on a local scale for millennia. Remains found in middens have been dated at twenty-five hundred years old. In the Commander Islands to the west, carved sea otter bones were employed in several games and used as ornaments. The penis bone was used as a powdered remedy for fever, and the fur was often mixed with a little sulphur to serve as tinder when lighting fires. Presumably the Aleuts valued the fur as winter clothing and bedding and may have eaten the flesh to complement their fish diet.

Hunters carried bone or soft stone charms carved in the likeness of their quarry that were said to make the sea otters more approachable. Kayaks built of a slender lath frame covered with sealskins were vital in hunting. About 13 feet (4 m) long and 1.5 feet (.5 m) across the beam, each kayak could carry two people. Usually several boats in a long line were employed in an otter hunt. As soon as the quarry was spotted, the nearest boat raised a paddle as a signal to the other crews. They all surrounded the spot, waiting for the animal to surface again. A quick shout sent it under before it had much time to draw breath, and the spot was surrounded by the boats again. The procedure was repeated until the otter was exhausted and could easily be speared. A mother with a young cub was especially easy prey. The spears were about 6 feet (2 m) long, carved from driftwood, painted red and decorated with otter hunting scenes. Each carried marks tallying the number of otters that it had killed. The barbed tip was of copper or bone and, being detachable, was attached to the shaft by a long line of leather thong. Thus, if a wounded otter tried to escape, it could be pulled into the boat and clubbed.

Netting was another common technique. The upper edge of the net was fitted at intervals with wooden floats carved as decoys in the form of sea otters lying on their backs. Otters became enmeshed and drowned. On rare occasions otters could be caught on shore. A chain of hunters along the tideline cut off the animals' retreat. In winter storms the noise of wind and waves allowed the men to approach a sleeping otter undetected and to dispatch it with a club. Not surprisingly, otters soon learned to avoid coming ashore.

In 1741, far to the north and eight years after Father Taraval had his historic encounter with otters in Baja California, Vitus Bering set sail from Okhotsk in Siberia. His ship flew the flag

The Fur Trade **35**

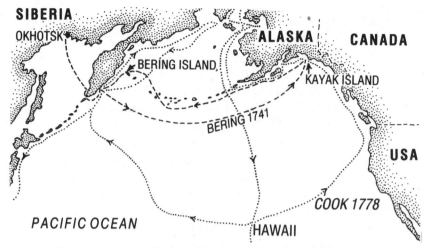

The voyages of Vitus Bering and Captain Cook

of Catherine the Great of Russia, its captain charged with exploring the resources of the straits that were soon to bear his name. On board he carried, as surgeon, the German naturalist Georg Wilhelm Steller. Bering made a landfall on the continent of North America (at Kayak Island in Alaska), where, in the one day he was allowed ashore, Steller made copious notes on flora and fauna and gathered numerous examples of North American arts and crafts. On the way home in November, through torrential rain, fog and storms, Bering's ship, the *St. Peter,* wrecked on one of the Commander Islands—later to be named after the explorer himself. His crew was wracked with scurvy, and thirty of them, together with the fifty-nine-year-old Bering, died and were buried there.

One of the first creatures they encountered was what they first thought was a bear or wolverine but which Steller recognized as a type of sea otter. "They covered the shore in great droves," he wrote. "They would come up to our fires, and would not be driven away until, after many of them had been slain, they learnt to know us and run away." The sailors soon recovered their health on the 55 pounds (25 kg) of flesh that each full-grown otter yielded. The meat was tough, but a young otter was "most delicious."

During the long winter nights, Bering's crew relieved their boredom by gambling, first for money, which was of course no use

36   Sea Otters

to them, and later for otter pelts. Steller admitted, "Such is the beauty of the animal and especially of its skin that this otter alone is incomparable and without equal, for in the amazing beauty and softness of its fur it surpasses all other creatures of the vast ocean."

The shipwrecked mariners also spent their time more profitably, building a boat to take them to safety. Eventually the craft was launched, but there was room to take only a small quantity of their newly discovered currency—eight hundred sea otter pelts. Nonetheless, back in civilization this precious cargo provided unparalleled impetus for Russian endeavors in the Arctic. Always voluptuous in her tastes, the expedition's patron, Catherine the Great, was overwhelmed by the new fur and at once commissioned a cloak to sweep from her throat to her ankles. Other Russian ships immediately were dispatched in pursuit of this exquisite new commodity, which they referred to as "soft gold."

In 1745, two ships landed on Bering Island and killed fifteen hundred otters; another expedition collected a similar harvest in the following two seasons. Not surprisingly, sea otters on Bering soon began to decline, so that by 1755, despite much effort on the part of the hunters, the island yielded only twenty furs. Attention then turned to the neighboring Mednyi Island, which was much more difficult to access. It quickly suffered a similar fate. In 1754, for example, 790 otters were taken there, but only twenty between 1760 and 1763. Thereafter, the Commander Islands were abandoned while the hunters exploited fresh pastures further east. The otters on both Bering and Mednyi Islands then enjoyed a little respite, but periodic ravages by hunters insured the animals never returned to even a fraction of their former abundance.

By 1760, sailings to the more distant Aleutian Islands had become both commonplace and profitable. In one season alone five Russian schooners accounted for no fewer than three thousand skins. A ready market was found at Canton in China. Having once occurred as far south as Hokkaido in Japan, the sea otter was already familiar to oriental aristocracy. Skins were made into full-length robes or else into belts and sashes, sometimes overlaid with pearls. Tails were much esteemed for hats, mittens and small trimmings. It was to Canton that the crew of Captain Cook's ship

The Fur Trade 37

Resolution brought the furs they had collected along the North American coast.

Captain James Cook had reached the forested shores of Vancouver Island early in 1778. Local natives offered for barter an array of animal skins, among them those of sea otters. Cook noted in his journal how the Native Americans adorned their flaxen garments with fringes of fur and frequently tied a sea otter, bear or wolf skin around their shoulders as a cloak. Farther north, near Nootka, Cook's journal continued, "Sea otters, which live mostly in the water, are found here. The fur of these animals, as mentioned in the Russian accounts, is certainly softer and finer than that of others we know of, and therefore the discovery of this part of the continent of North America, where so valuable an article of commerce may be met with, cannot be a matter of indifference." A gross understatement perhaps, but certainly prophetic.

After a severe gale, Cook touched land again north of what is now Juneau in Alaska (at a point he was relieved to name Cape Fairweather). He proceeded past Kayak Island to Sandwich Sound (later renamed Prince William Sound), where he encountered Eskimos clothed in skins of sea otters and other mammals. A full-length cloak would consist of three good otter skins sewn together in a square and loosely tied over the shoulders with small leather strings. On the Aleutian island of Unalaska the *Resolution* met with some Russians, one of whom offered Cook a sea otter skin as a present that, it was claimed, was worth eighty rubles at Kamchatka. Cook noted how there were Russians "settled on all the principal islands between Oonalaska and Kamchatka, for the sole purpose of collecting furs. Their great object is the sea beaver or otter. I never heard them inquire after any other animal, though those whose skins are of inferior value are also made part of their cargo."

Cook and his crew accumulated many otter skins from the natives before turning south in 1779 to the island of Hawaii in the South Pacific, where the good captain was killed. Later the *Resolution* and a sister ship were to return north to Canton, where the furs were sold. "The rage with which our seamen were possessed to return to Cook's River (near Prince William Sound) and, with another cargo of skins make their fortunes, was not far short of mutiny," commented the *Resolution*'s acting captain. "The barter

38   Sea Otters

Cook's Resolution *and*
Discovery *in Prince William Sound*

which had been carrying on with the Chinese for our sea otter skins, had procured a very whimsical change in the dress of all our crew. On our arrival here nothing could exceed the ragged appearance both of the younger officers and seamen.... European clothes had been long worn out, or patched up with skins.... These were now again mixed and eked out with the gaudiest silks and cottons of China."

Like the effect of Bering's expedition forty years earlier on Russian hunters, Cook's journals released a flood of commercial interest in the otter trade among British, American, French and Portuguese trapper ships. The "soft gold" rush had begun.

While Russia controlled the fur trade in Alaska, Spain monopolized sea otter hunting farther south in its territories of California and Mexico. In 1786, Spain negotiated a treaty with China. In exchange for quicksilver (vital for Spain's silver-mining operations in Mexico), the Chinese were promised 20,000 sea otter pelts annually. However, in the first three months of 1787, only 1,060 were acquired for export. To improve the returns, the Spaniards made the goods for barter with the local Indians more attractive and brought skilled hunters from Europe. By November, another 1,750 otter skins were being shipped. But success remained poor because control of the trade had been removed from the local missions to Spanish soldiers who badly abused the Indians. Enthusiasm among the professional hunters also ebbed.

Spain tried to tighten up the arrangement so that by 1790 nearly 10,000 otter pelts and some seal skins had been shipped to Canton—equivalent to over $3 million of quicksilver.

After the publication of Captain Cook's journals in 1790, English merchantmen began to cash in on the act. Spain managed to resist such incursions until Boston merchant ships joined in. Ostensibly, they called at Spanish North American ports only to take on provisions, but they really sought illicit sea otter pelts. The Indians responded no more to the American approaches than they had to Spain's. Nonetheless, efforts had to be made to stop this contraband.

The Russians were having much more success in the pursuit of sea otters farther north, mainly due to the special hunting skills of the Aleuts. Professional Russian fur traders—called *promyshlenniki*— brutally exploited the natives to the point of slavery. Aleut women and children were taken hostage and any of the men who refused to hunt for their Russian masters were tortured or shot. The Aleut communities were also being decimated by disease. At one time, Fox Island alone supported 10,000 to 12,000 Aleuts, but by 1790 their numbers had dwindled to only 1,900.

By 1783, Russia had established its first base on the North American continent—on Kodiak Island in Alaska. Three years later Gerassim Pribilof discovered a group of islands to the north that came to bear his name. He returned with no fewer than 2,325 sea otter skins, worth 150 rubles, or $50 each. Three sailors who were left ashore on the Pribilofs that year killed five thousand otters. Not surprisingly, the following season's harvest was only one thousand, and within six years the sea otter was almost extinct—following exactly the pattern that had prevailed upon the Commander Islands several decades earlier.

However, the Pribilofs also had the largest known colony of fur seals, numbered in the millions. Although the skins were worth only 3 rubles ($1 each), fur seal carcasses could be rendered down for their valuable oil, providing a resource that the Russians could not ignore. The islands were uninhabited, so Aleut families from Fox Island were forcibly relocated there to carry out the slaughter. In the first year, they accounted for 40,000 fur seals. Killing them was easy while the seals were ashore for breeding, and the Russian warehouses were soon bulging with rotting unsold skins. In 1803, some 700,000 out of a hoard of 800,000 pelts were thrown away as useless.

But the fur seal trade is another story. The insatiable thirst for the fabulous sea otter fur pushed the *promyshlenniki* from the Aleutians to the Alaskan mainland and southward along this seemingly limitless shoreline. In 1799, the Russian American Company was formed under imperial charter, and a base was established at New Archangel (now known as Sitka). The notorious Alexander Baranov—the "Lord of Alaska"—became its first governor, and he soon earned another nickname, "The Little Tzar," for his autocratic management. In 1804, a single one of Baranov's ships landed a bumper cargo of 15,000 otter skins. At that time the Unalaska district alone was still yielding about one thousand pelts annually, but by 1826 only fifteen were taken. This was typical of the situation elsewhere, and Baranov realized that the free-for-all could not be allowed to persist. He strove to introduce conservation measures and, no doubt, being a man of strong will, he achieved some success in insuring they were adhered to. The coast from the Aleutians to Prince William Sound on the Alaskan mainland was divided into districts, and quotas were set with a proviso that only male otters were to be killed. For a time, hunting was permitted for only two years and then halted for three. Sealing was also brought to an end temporarily.

By this time the Americans were keen to set up their own sea otter venture and approached Baranov for the loan of some Aleut hunters. He was understandably reluctant. Poaching by foreign ships was a nuisance, and he had enough on his hands subduing the local Indians. In 1802, for instance, his Sitka settlement had been attacked and nearly wiped out. However, Baranov also appreciated that the northern otter grounds were being depleted at an alarming rate, and the company would soon have to extend its operations much further south, thus encroaching on foreign territory. His ships did not have the long-distance capability of the American vessels, and the company would benefit from a base further south. So he agreed to release some Aleut hunters in return for arms to fight off the Indians, together with an option on setting up a trading post in northern California.

The Fur Trade **41**

The Spaniards of course bitterly resented incursions by foreign boats and took action whenever possible. In the autumn of 1810, for instance, they succeeded in capturing several Aleut hunters in San Francisco Bay and killed a few others. But the Russian American Company decided it was worth taking up its option, and in 1812 Fort Russ (later anglicized to "Ross") was founded, some 65 miles (100 km) north of San Francisco. From here the Russians hoped to negotiate a settlement with Spain, but their approaches met with such a frosty response that they continued poaching in the meantime.

In 1817, Spain finally agreed to a treaty with Russia. This permitted access to San Francisco Bay, with the anticipated annual crop of 20,000 sea otter pelts being divided equally between both parties. Spain was again guilty of undue optimism. The Californian yield had peaked in 1811 (with a crop of 9,356 skins), and the sea otters were now declining. Furthermore, the Yankee traders were having a particularly hard time for a variety of reasons—the War of Independence, a British blockade off Canton, Russian efforts to shrug off their American partners and the Mexican revolution against Spain.

With hunting in southern California easing off, the otters recovered somewhat until beaver trappers arrived from the north. They introduced the practice of shooting otters both from the shore and from boats. One man, Isaac Sparks, started with only a rifle—having to swim out to retrieve his prizes. He was soon able to afford to hire a swimmer and then to build a small boat, eventually forming a partnership to charter a small schooner.

The hunting methods of these American gunmen differed from those of the Aleuts with their spears. Some of the shooting was done from the land—even if otters on the sea were still well out of range. The noise of the surf usually drowned out the shots. The hunter would then wait for the tide to wash the carcasses ashore. Some men succeeded in improving their line of sight over the waves by sitting on a light, portable stepladder set on the beach. One authority has estimated that even the best marksman averaged twenty-five shots for every otter obtained, and then only half the carcasses killed were ever retrieved; they might drift out to sea or else be picked off the strandline later by someone else.

Fort Ross, California

Most of the hunting, however, was carried out at sea by small groups of three to twelve men in small, clinker-built ex-whaling boats. As an example of the success rate, one boat in 1831 collected 150 otter pelts in its first six days. The poachers devised various means to bypass Mexico's regulations—by taking out Mexican citizenship or marrying local women. They were ruthless to the natives and often helped themselves to the natives' cattle and horses along the coast. The Mexican authorities proved powerless to control them. The situation finally resolved itself when otters became harder to find. By this time the Russians too were losing interest. Fort Ross was abandoned in 1841. It has recently been restored as a tourist attraction—and a sad monument to the slaughter that brought the sea otter to the verge of extinction.

At this point sea otters were so scarce that they were not worth the effort involved in hunting or trapping them, although some hunting carried on into the 1840s. In 1848, Mexico finally conceded California to the United States. The following year gold was discovered in the Sierra Nevada foothills. By a whisker Mexico had missed out on the fabulous profits of a new gold rush. Most of the American otter hunters abandoned the soft gold on the coast to seek real gold in the hills.

Farther north the stage was set for another major political transaction in which the sea otter trade again played no small part—the addition of Russian Alaska to the United States. It has been estimated that between 1740 and 1790 about 250,000 sea otters had been slaughtered in the North Pacific, worth at least $50 million to the Russians and their competitors. This figure does not include those otters killed and never retrieved, poorly prepared skins that had to be discarded or the otters that had been illegally poached. In the last five years of their presence in Alaska, the Russians had harvested only 11,137 skins. However, one authority has estimated that during the entire 126 years of the Russian occupation of Alaska, around 1 million sea otters were slain by all nations. In 1867, the territory was no longer considered a commercial proposition and was finally sold to the United States.

However, there were still otters to be had, and in the next four years the Americans found 12,208. From 1871 to 1880 at least 40,283 more were killed, and a further 47,842 were killed in the following decade. By now the American-owned Alaska Commercial Company monopolized the fur trade. In the last decade of the nineteenth century, however, it handled only 6,143 sea otter pelts. Nonetheless, it has been claimed that over the next forty years, Alaska was to yield enough seal and otter skins to offset the $7.2 million with which the Americans had purchased the state.

By 1911, it is reckoned that only five hundred to one thousand sea otters remained alive, scattered in thirteen small, isolated populations—on the Kurile Islands, Kamchatka, the Commanders, a few of the Aleutians, two places on the Alaska peninsula, Queen Charlotte Island in British Columbia, central California and the Mexican Benito Island. In 1911, the Fur Seal Treaty was signed by the United States, Britain, Russia and Japan—protective legislation that included the sea otter. In 1913, the Preservation and Protection of Fur Seals and Sea Otters became federal law in America. That year also saw the Aleutian Islands declared a national wildlife refuge.

At the turn of the twentieth century, the Commander Islands, not part of Russia's Alaskan package to the United States, had been leased to various fur companies, ending with the Kamchatka Hunting Company. A limited sea otter cull was permit-

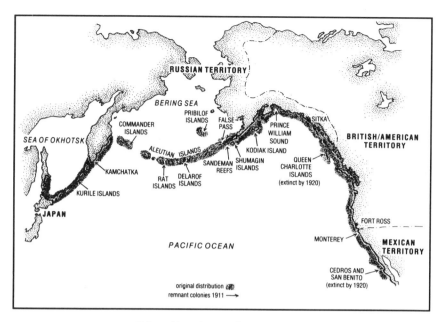

RUSSIAN TERRITORY

BERING SEA

PRIBILOF ISLANDS
COMMANDER ISLANDS
FALSE PASS
SITKA
PRINCE WILLIAM SOUND
BRITISH/AMERICAN TERRITORY
SEA OF OKHOTSK
ALEUTIAN ISLANDS
KODIAK ISLAND
SANDEMAN REEFS
SHUMAGIN ISLANDS
QUEEN CHARLOTTE ISLANDS (extinct by 1920)
KAMCHATKA
RAT ISLANDS
DELAROF ISLANDS
KURILE ISLANDS
JAPAN
FORT ROSS
MONTEREY
MEXICAN TERRITORY
PACIFIC OCEAN
CEDROS AND SAN BENITO (extinct by 1920)

original distribution
remnant colonies 1911 →

Distribution of sea otters
before and after commercial hunting

ted, amounting to about two hundred animals per year. This was later reduced to eighty per annum, then forty, until in 1924 hunting sea otters on the Commanders was banned altogether. Because the otters were so scarce, prices for their furs had reached an all-time high, and poachers, especially the Japanese, were a constant threat. They often employed barbaric methods, pouring oil on waters near shore, or kerosene, creosote and other malodorous substances on rocks where the otters gathered. The disoriented animals were then driven out to sea, where they could be easily shot. Poachers also worked the shores of North America and finally caused the extinction in 1920 of the colonies on Queen Charlotte Island and on Benito Island.

Poaching continued in Alaska until, in 1936, the U.S. Bureau of Fisheries stationed agents at Amchitka to protect the wildlife, and otters in particular. During the Second World War, the sea otter finally began to increase—subsequently by about 15 percent per annum. By the 1950s, it was no longer considered endangered. Anticipating a demand for sea otter furs, the U.S. Fish and Wildlife Service began a long-term study of the species in 1954

The Fur Trade **45**

and instigated experimental harvests in 1962, 1963 and 1967. On January 30, 1968, one thousand sea otter pelts were available for public auction in Seattle, Washington. Few of the traders had ever set eyes on a sea otter skin. "The fur was clearly of the finest quality and of great value." Another fifteen hundred were marketed over the next two years until, by 1970, lack of funds, and to some extent lack of interest, slowed the culling program. Fortunately, the Marine Mammal Protection Act of 1972 gave the animal full legal protection again in the United States.

The sea otter is still scarce in many parts of its range, and Alaska holds some 90 percent of the world population. It is estimated that upward of seven thousand sea otters now live around the Kurile Islands and a further three thousand or more along the Kamchatka coast. The Commander Islands contain about 2,500 (900 to 1,200 on Mednyi and the remainder on Bering).

The Russians claim that the sea otter's entire historical range has now been reoccupied, and the species now enjoys full protection. There are no conflicts with local fisheries, but in the future some limited hunting for furs may be permitted, a process that is claimed to reduce population fluctuations and eliminate sick animals—rather spurious reasons to a conservationist.

The species now occurs throughout most of the Aleutian Islands (where they might number 10,000 to 20,000, though no recent census has been undertaken) and along much of the Alaskan peninsula (nearly 20,000 in 1986). Three thousand individuals were counted on the Kodiak archipelago in 1984 and over five thousand in Prince William Sound (both counts are probably underestimations). There remains an extensive stretch of coast south through British Columbia, Washington, Oregon and northern California that has remained devoid of sea otters since the nineteenth century. Attempts to reintroduce the species at several localities there in recent years will be described later. The tiny population surviving in central California first attracted media attention in 1938 and after varying fortunes has increased, albeit slowly, to 1,864 by 1989. But clearly sea otters have not yet recovered fully from the holocaust they suffered in the last century.

4

Sex Life, Birth and Death

ea otters are sociable creatures and, when not foraging, usually associate together in groups called rafts. In Alaska, rafts of two thousand individuals have been recorded, but they are normally much smaller than this. Groups are usually of one sex, male rafts being larger (in Alaska up to one hundred animals on average), while those of the females number only ten to thirty. An average male group in California was found to be twenty-seven, and female groups less than twenty.

Some males occupy a territory all the year round, especially if food is abundant there and the all-male rafts are too far for them to commute. Other males will leave the raft to occupy the same territory in successive breeding seasons, waiting for females in heat to pass through. By definition, a territory is an area that is actively defended. One Alaskan male occupied the entrance and central portion of a small lagoon, with only one potential rival living along the edge. He chased his neighbor frequently, porpoising in pursuit up to their mutual boundary. Only once when the dominant male relaxed to turn back did his opponent pluck up the courage to instigate an attack. They lunged with open mouths, each trying to bite the other's head and neck. There was one other brief fight when the subdominant otter found his retreat cut off by the observer's boat. But this unusual aggression seems to have been imposed by the confined situation within the small lagoon. In reality fighting is very rare in Alaska and uncommon in Califor-

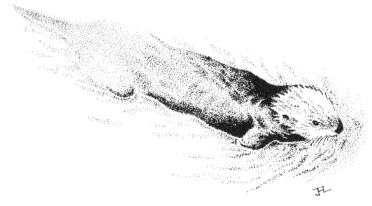

Sea otter swimming

Sex Life, Birth and Death **49**

nia. One Monterey scientist witnessed only two disputes during his studies, only one being territorial.

A third group of males do not seem to hold permanent territories but instead join rafting females for a few days while in search of a mate. The male at first swims around on his belly, occasionally stopping to sit high in the water and look around. In Alaska, males may sometimes venture ashore, sniffing around the favored hauling-out rocks of females.

CALIFORNIAN SEA OTTERS ASHORE

While it is not unusual to see Alaskan sea otters hauled out on a beach or on rocks, it is distinctly rare to see their Californian cousins do so. However, there is some evidence that the habit might be becoming more common.

In March 1970, a naturalist unrolled his sleeping bag on a beach near Monterey to spend a memorable, if fitful, night at the side of a dozy sea otter, which he nicknamed "Hopkins." The creature moved even closer to him to avoid the flowing tide. At frequent intervals Hopkins raised his head or shook himself. He lay on his tummy but sometimes rolled over to rub his back in the sand. For long periods he lay motionless, however, and at 5:00 A.M. he returned to the sea. This was to become such a regular nightly routine over the next eighteen months that the naturalist was able to make a unique collection of two hundred otter feces (or scats) for later analysis. Crab remains were detected in 81 percent of them, mussel fragments in 54 percent and squid in 30 percent.

Several other apparently healthy otters were seen ashore along the Monterey coast in April 1973; one near the car park at the famous Cypress Point beauty spot permitted photographers to approach within 6 feet (2 m). That September two otters were seen sparring with one another on an offshore rock. A third tried to join them but was washed off by a wave. It then sought the company of some harbor seals on another rock nearby, but they moved off. So the friendly

50   Sea Otters

otter tried a young elephant seal but changed its mind when it was greeted by bared teeth. As many as five otters were subsequently seen hauled out with seals that summer, and, quite recently, fourteen adult sea otters and four cubs came ashore near Point Lobos.

Volunteers now often mount guard on beached otters to prevent them being molested by humans or stray dogs. Once or twice a sea otter has even taken over an inflatable raft temporarily vacated by swimmers and may be reluctant to abandon its comforts when the rightful owner returns. Otters may well come ashore more frequently in spring while the kelp is sparse, and estrous females may seek to avoid the attentions of amorous males (although some enthusiastic suitors may be tempted ashore, too).

It has been common to find sick or moribund sea otters on beaches, but on January 16, 1987, one was found in the middle of a plowed field near a Moss Landing farm. Appropriately nicknamed "Old Macdonald," he weighed only 47 pounds (21 kg) and his teeth were worn or missing. He was released into the harbor the next day but was found suffering from a bleeding nose and some broken hind toes on April 20. A month later, having put on 12 pounds (5 kg), he was found shot—the ultimate betrayal of his misguided trust in man.

When a male locates a likely female in the water, he approaches from below and tries to grasp her under the armpits with his forepaws. Or else he surfaces beside her, rubbing or sniffing at her body, especially her rear end. If she is not receptive, she turns away, pushing or snapping at him in irritation. The disgruntled, rejected male might then salvage his damaged pride by snatching away any food the female may have.

If she is in breeding condition, the pair may roll and frolic together on the surface, nuzzling and fondling each other for up to an hour. Suddenly she becomes submissive and lies rigid, belly up, paws held stiffly upright and back slightly bowed. The male lies beneath her and grasps her chest from behind with his front paws. He then reaches over her head and bites her on the nose! Understandably, the female shrieks and gurgles, seemingly finding difficulty in breathing. Despite her struggles, the male may hang

Nose scars in female sea otters

on to her for up to an hour, biting her hard several times before copulation is achieved. Thus the female often emerges from this tortured encounter with a gashed and bleeding nose, which may develop a conspicuous pink scar. While this might be expected to do little to enhance her beauty, scientists find characteristically shaped scars useful in telling individual female sea otters apart. Indeed, it may be quite a fashion, with up to 60 percent of female sea otters possessing pink scars on their noses. On the other hand, such wounds can become infected, and at least one poor female is known to have died from a nasty nasal ulcer.

The thick tail makes successful dorsal mounting difficult, and the male has to twist his lower body athletically to enter the female successfully. One copulation lasted fourteen minutes. When the animals separate, they each groom themselves and may even fall asleep together. On one occasion a male mated with the same female again half an hour later. Otherwise, the male may move off to locate another female in heat. All copulations witnessed in the wild have taken place on the water. If the female still has her well-grown cub as chaperon, the jealous youngster may well sabotage the male's chances of achieving a successful coupling. Matings take place at any time of the year, but in the western Pacific, Russian biologists report two peak breeding periods in June and July and September and October. This latter peak occurs only in Alaskan waters, while July to October is favored in Califor-

52   Sea Otters

nia. Alaskan males who hold better quality territories (in terms of food abundance and shelter) are reckoned to achieve more copulations, presumably with a succession of different females.

Females are usually three or four years old when they first become sexually mature. Males may reach maturity at about five but usually need another few years before they make their first successful attempts at breeding.

Males are of course larger than females—several pounds heavier and on average some 4 inches (10 cm) longer in the body. Young males and females can be difficult to distinguish in the field unless one can make out the bulge around the male's penis or the abdominal teats of the female. Older males tend to have larger heads and thicker necks than females. A cub lying on the stomach of an otter is a sure sign that it is the mother, as males have never been known to offer their offspring a ride. Being relatively long lived, with a fifteen- or twenty-year average lifespan (females are longer lived than males), sea otters have a long reproductive life. The method of determining age by using cementum layers in teeth, so useful amongst other mammals, is not reliable for otters, probably because their maritime environment lacks the seasonal extremes that cause the laying down of distinct annual rings in the teeth. The oldest known wild female was reckoned to be twenty-three years of age, the oldest known male, eighteen. A captive male that was at least nineteen recently died at the Vancouver Aquarium; his teeth were worn and decayed and he was blind, so he would never have reached such a venerable age in the wild. (Nonetheless, this grizzled old veteran was still able to father offspring in his twilight years.)

Sexual Dimorphism in Alaskan Sea Otters		
	adult males	*adult females*
Mean weight	61 pounds (28 kg)	48 pounds (22 kg)
Maximum weight	99 pounds (45 kg)	72 pounds (32.5 kg)
Mean length	53 inches (135 cm)	49 inches (125 cm)
Maximum length	58 inches (148 cm)	55 inches (140 cm)
Number measured	79	254

Sex Life, Birth and Death **53**

The period from copulation to the birth of the cub is called gestation. There is some debate as to how long this actually is in the case of sea otters, and it appears to be highly variable. Gestation is probably about four months, but in some females it appears to last much longer, often eight months and sometimes up to twelve months. This variation is probably achieved by delaying implantation in the uterine wall of the fertilized egg (after which its development can begin). Such delayed implantation occurs commonly in such mammals as badgers and seals. The river otter normally produces two cubs, which are blind and scarcely mobile at birth, after a gestation period of two months. Because of its totally aquatic lifestyle, the sea otter must produce a cub that is larger and further developed. Almost invariably it produces only one, so why its gestation should be so much longer still remains something of a mystery. The accepted position at the moment seems to be that the sea otter has a gestation of about four months coupled with a delayed implant that may last from a few days to a few months, a period that can be extended if necessary.

Births can take place in any month of the year, but in Alaska and Russia the harsh winter tends to be avoided, with minor peaks occurring in May and June. In the more equable climate of California, sea otters tend to give birth from January to March, avoiding the late spring and early summer when strong winds prevail.

Nearly all births take place at sea, and rarely has the event been witnessed. A Russian biologist was lucky on two counts, seeing not only a birth but one which took place on dry land. On January 8, 1932, he was watching four otters just offshore. One of them seemed distinctly uneasy, agitatedly swimming around some small boulders. "At 11:25 it climbed a rock and rested a long time in a hollow. Vigorous restless motions continued for two hours. At 1:30 a very light, newborn sea otter, as big as a cat, appeared in its paws. The mother, lying on her back, licked it vigorously, and held it to her chest or belly. At 2:20 one of the three distant sea otters swam to the stone. As soon as it ascended, the mother hastily climbed down and disappeared."

The naturalist Georg Steller and many Aleut hunters believed that sea otters normally gave birth on dry land. Half of the fetuses found in dead otters are oriented for birth headfirst—just as in fur seals, which also pup on land. On the other hand, cetaceans, which calve in the water, always give birth tail first. So in the past, even in Steller's time, it may well have been normal practice for sea otters to cub ashore. But now it is a rare occurrence—perhaps a response to man's constant harassment—and nearly all births occur at sea.

A BIRTH ASHORE IN CALIFORNIA

On February 20, 1981, a young naturalist was watching a lone female sea otter in a sheltered cove near Point Lobos, California. The otter ventured onto some rocks about 3 yards (2.7 m) offshore—an interesting observation in its own right. But then she began behaving oddly. Standing on all fours, she moved her head around, lay on her left side, stretched out her neck and rested it on the rock. Occasionally she would curl round to peer at her tail. A minute or two later she appeared to be pulling wet strands of membrane over her belly and then could be seen licking a new-born cub held in her forepaws. Licking off the clinging membranes, she groomed vigorously for half an hour, turning it from side to side as it lay across her chest. The cub's eyes were open, its fur standing in wet, spiky tufts as it submitted to its mother's attentions. The female then became very still, resting or else nursing her baby. After ten minutes, she resumed grooming.

This had been the first observation of a Californian sea otter giving birth in the wild, and it has usually been assumed that the event takes place in the water—as has been seen among captive otters. There is, however, another, Russian, observation of a birth on land, which is mentioned on page 54.

Almost invariably a single cub is born. When one scientist undertook postmortems on no fewer than 1,360 female sea otters,

Sea otter with very young cub

he found only five twin fetuses—and one set of triplets—all well developed. Instances of twins being born are very rare (and certainly never triplets). One dead female was near full term and carried two cubs, but they were well below average weight, and, being premature, they probably contributed to the death of the mother. In cases of twins being born it is unlikely that both cubs will survive.

It is also rare for sea otters to breed successfully in captivity. When they do, first-time mothers tend to show a higher incidence of stillbirths. However, they exhibit a greater degree of success with each successive birth, probably something that also happens in the wild.

Three Californian scientists observed the behavior of an otter immediately after giving birth. It was 11 A.M. on a February morning in 1970 when a female sea otter was spotted on the water with a newborn cub. The cub's fur was wet, and the mother licked it vigorously for two and a half hours. By this time the little one was dry and perfectly fluffy. The mother then tidied herself up a bit before subjecting the cub to another hour and a quarter of wash and brush up. The cub could be seen making weak head movements—no doubt in protest at such maternal attention! It first sucked at 2:53 P.M., feeding for eight minutes while its mother licked its rear end. The pup was then placed on the water where, because of the meticulous grooming, it floated like a feather. Its mother allowed it to drift no more than a yard away while she attended to her own fur.

A captive female at San Diego spent a similar time grooming her newborn cub and also first suckled it four hours after the birth; another cub, however, was not seen to take its first milk for twelve hours. For the next few days, the youngster will feed every few hours, for five to ten minutes at a time.

 **BREEDING IN CAPTIVITY**

By 1980, ten sea otters had been born at Point Defiance Zoo and Aquarium near Tacoma, Washington, but sadly none survived longer than sixty-three days. In this same period six cubs were born at Sea World in San Diego, California, three of which were stillbirths. On June 4, 1979, Jenny, one of six females penned with a single male called Tiger, gave birth to a cub. Although she appeared to tend it well, mother and baby had to be isolated from the other females when they began to make a nuisance of themselves. The cub died after twenty-one days, the longest any San Diego pup had so far survived. Her next offspring was born on January 29, 1980, but died two days later.

At 4:30 P.M. on May 16, 1979, however, one of Seattle's three females, called Etika (about six years old), gave birth to her first cub. Almost immediately she took it on her chest and began grooming it. Even while it sucked, she licked its tail and hind legs. The cub, a male called Tichuk, made his first attempts to groom himself at two weeks. After a month he could dive underwater, if only a few feet. By mid-October, Tichuk was almost as big as his mother and would almost sink her when he clambered onto her chest. Although still not fully weaned, by consuming 3.3 pounds (1.5 kg) of solid food a day and weighing 12 to 13 pounds (5 to 6 kg), he was obviously eating enough solid food to sustain himself—some of it stolen from others.

Indeed, Tichuk proved something of a delinquent, annoying the other otters by splashing them, pouncing on them or colliding with them as he swam. He often tried to associate with his father, Tak, but his mother disapproved. At a year old Tichuk armed himself with a rock and set about

Sex Life, Birth and Death **57**

dismantling the underwater lights, wiring, drains and other equipment in his pool. He removed bolts and sealing strips from the pool's glass front, drilled holes in its concrete edges and even managed to open the door of his cage. When Etika gave birth to another cub on August 31, 1980, Tichuk was so eager to play with it that he had to be removed to a separate enclosure, with a tolerant female called Kiska for company.

At 4 P.M. on January 12, 1983, an Alaskan sea otter in Vancouver Aquarium gave birth to a male cub. She turned and rolled his wet, limp form in her forepaws as she licked and blew his fur dry. He grew fluffier by the minute and was seen to suck for the first time sixteen hours later. Clamchops, as he came to be known, was another hyperactive baby, and on April 29 that same year another female, Sanya, gave birth to a little playmate for him. Others have since been born at Vancouver, one coming to an untimely end at eight months, when it got caught in the grate at the bottom of its pool and drowned.

The mother may not eat at all that first day because, when she dives, she has to leave her vulnerable youngster at the surface unattended. Unless it is asleep it mews piteously like a young seagull until she reappears. If the female is alarmed she may clutch her little one to her breast and take it with her under the water. She cannot do this too frequently, of course, for she risks drowning the poor creature. Sea otters are fearless in defense of their cubs, as the Indian and Aleut hunters knew only too well. Despite his own desperate circumstances, the shipwrecked Georg Steller could find time to admire the maternal habits of sea otters. "When they sleep at sea," he wrote in his journal, "they fold their young in their arms, just as human mothers do their babes. . . . They embrace their young with an affection that is scarcely credible." Sea otter mothers have been known to carry a dead pup for days before finally discarding it.

One Californian sea otter mother had particular problems with her newborn twins. She was watched for two days with her unusual brood, which were reckoned to be no more than a day or two old. She could only let each cub sit on her chest for half the

Sea otter with cub

usual time that other mothers carried their cubs. At first she was careful not to let the unlucky one float too far from her reach. If any other otters showed too much interest, she would move away carrying one pup on her chest and holding the other in her mouth. Nor could she groom each one for as long as normal, and over the two days she was not seen to forage for food at all. Suckling bouts were similarly half the normal time and, as there did not seem to be enough room at her teats for both, she frequently had to switch cubs from her chest to the water.

On the second day she groomed more attentively but already seemed to act as though she had only one cub. The other drifted away in the wind. When it was 15 yards (14 m) off, she finally went to retrieve it, still carrying the first cub. She then set this one in the water while she gathered up the other to groom it. The first then drifted off and was ignored until, eventually, it was washed ashore .25 mile (.5 km) away. Having to accept that the poor mother could only cope with one youngster, the scientists watching on the shore rescued the abandoned drifter. It was an unusually small female, with the umbilical cord still attached. The cub weighed only 2.5 pounds (1.1 kg), but after ten months in the Monterey Aquarium, where it was affectionately named "Milkdud," it weighed a healthy 33 pounds (15 kg). A similar instance has been recorded in Alaska, but it was eventually concluded that the mother had temporarily adopted an orphan; she only ever allowed one cub, presumably her own, to suck.

Sex Life, Birth and Death **59**

At birth a sea otter cub weighs around 4.5 pounds (2 kg) and is covered in a woolly, light brown to yellowish fur. Mothers usually remain separate from other otters, and the only aggression they may show to each other seems to be when they are forced to shelter close together during strong winds. With a small cub, a mother spends little time foraging, sometimes no more than 2 percent of her day. Another 10 percent of her time is spent grooming herself and 20 percent grooming her youngster, such bouts lasting up to fifty minutes or more. Eight percent of the day is spent in nursing, averaging six sucking bouts a day, each of about nine minutes.

At five days old one captive cub was left alone by its mother for only eighty-two minutes in twenty-four hours. The next day the cub was making crude swimming motions, always on its belly, and on the seventh day the mother started taking it underwater when she dived, but never for longer than a minute at a time. On this day the cub first groomed itself. When three and a half weeks old, it may spend up to 15 percent of its day in this activity, but even at several months old a youngster might not escape the attentions of its mother. At four or five weeks a cub will be swimming about actively on its own and may make its first attempts at diving. But it will not begin swimming on its back until

Mother and cub

60   *Sea Otters*

it is six to eight weeks old, its well-groomed fur making it so buoyant that even a determined youngster has difficulty getting completely underwater. It will still be permitted to ride on its mother's chest from time to time, but by the ninth week it is keen to accompany her underwater. Three weeks later a youngster's dives can average forty-five seconds, with the longest over one hundred seconds—well within the capabilities of an adult. By its thirteenth week the cub's fur has changed to a darker, more uniform brown color.

Although a very young cub may sample a little solid food, for the first month it still receives over 90 percent of its nourishment at its mother's teats. A sea otter's milk is very rich in fat, resembling that of cetaceans and seals more than its terrestrial mustelid relatives. A cub usually takes its first substantial solid meal at six weeks, thereafter soliciting more and more food from its mother until it begins finding its own. The young otter can be fully independent at about six months, when it weighs anything from 22 to 44 pounds (10 to 20 kg).

A few tagged females have been recorded reuniting with their cubs for short periods after weaning. One cub was seen about 5 miles (8 km) away from its mother, but three days later they were back together again. She then nursed and groomed it for another week or so before they finally parted for good. Another female had weaned her cub, then mated before meeting up with it again ten days later. She cared for it for another six weeks before finally rejecting it to mate with a different male. This was one of the longest dependency periods yet noted, no less than ten months long.

Although they have to provide such a prolonged period of parental care, most Californian females seem perfectly capable of producing another youngster the following season. No. 41, for instance, was tagged as a mature female near Pacific Grove on August 15, 1976. On January 8 she was spotted with a newborn cub. Eight months later the offspring was independent and No. 41 had a swollen nose from a gruelling mating encounter. She gave birth on February 28, 1978, less than five months after weaning her previous cub, which itself became independent eight months later. No. 41 had a new cub one to two months old by March 1979, but this cub disappeared by July—at three to five months old it may have become independent or else died. Its mother did not become pregnant again until November 1980, when she sported a newly healed nose scar.

In the northern waters of Alaska and Russia, the period of a cub's dependence upon its mother may be longer than in California—up to a year—so that some females might only be able to give birth every other year.

The first winter is, of course, a difficult time for young otters. Many are unable to find sufficient food on their own and consequently starve. One estimate is that 38 percent of cubs may die before weaning, especially if their mother is inexperienced. They may also become fatally chilled if their fur becomes at all soiled. The carcasses are washed ashore, where, in Alaska, they are readily scavenged by bald eagles. By early summer the eagles ignore such pickings and take more live prey. Young sea otters left temporarily unattended by their mothers are, of course, very vulnerable to eagles and, in the shallows, even to coyotes. Between 1969 and 1975 one team of ornithologists found no less than a hundred sea otter cubs in eagle eyries—10 to 20 percent of all the prey items recorded. Since young otters would be the equivalent of an eider or a cormorant in weight, they would constitute a significant proportion of the eagle's diet. Nonetheless, it is unlikely that the bald eagles were having a serious effect on the sea otter populations; they never killed adult otters. Other cubs are taken by sharks and killer whales. Sharks' teeth have been found embedded in bodies of sea otters, while additional victims may have been wrongly marked up as casualties of boat propellers. Within two and a half months in spring 1987, no fewer than seven shark-killed otters were found in California; an eighth recuperated in Monterey Aquarium before being released.

KILLER WHALES AND SEA OTTERS

Although there is a Russian account of killer whales killing a sea otter, in the majority of encounters the species ignore one another. A furry sea otter represents a pretty small

62   Sea Otters

meal for a 5-ton killer, and a pretty high-fiber one at that. In early April 1972, two whales were observed swimming off Monterey Peninsula, within 200 feet (60 m) of a raft of fifty sea otters. The whales passed within 30 feet (10 m) of another sea otter that was asleep in a kelp bed and remained blissfully unaware of any potential danger as it bobbed up and down in their wake. A second otter nearby showed much more interest, however, treading water to raise itself upright to get a better look. (Later the killer whales were seen to kill and eat two young sea lions and an immature elephant seal, so they obviously had been hungry.) On other occasions groups of otters have been seen swimming rapidly to the shore to avoid small pods of killers. It is not unreasonable that sea otters should maintain a healthy respect for killer whales, but obviously they are not a significant prey. Perhaps the whales find it difficult to successfully locate and hunt sea otters in dense kelp beds.

If a female is finding it hard to find food in rough weather, she may be forced to abandon a well-grown cub—especially where high densities of sea otters result in food being more thinly spread. The youngster will almost certainly starve to death, and even the mother herself may succumb. A younger cub makes fewer demands and so, being cared for adequately, both the cub and its mother have a better chance of survival. Age and body size also influence mortality in other ways. Although the sex ratio at birth is approximately equal, slightly more young males than females are picked up dead in an Alaskan winter. A male cub, being larger in body size, will require more food, so its stressed mother may abandon it more readily than she would a female cub.

One estimate suggests that 50 percent of juveniles may die before becoming independent. Only half of those that survive this period may then see the end of their first year, but this proportion may vary from place to place and from year to year. Adults, of course, have better survival prospects, only 10 to 30 percent dying each year. Full-grown sea otters picked up dead on a beach usually display worn or defective teeth, which must have affected their ability to find adequate food, especially in winter. Cases of disease are also known, and otters can also suffer injury in particularly

Sex Life, Birth and Death **63**

rough seas or during mating fights. Although rare amongst sea otters, territorial males have been seen fending off a neighbor. The rivals face each other, vigorously treading water to keep upright, while they box with their forepaws. At the end of each round the adversaries face away before retreating to their respective corners. Individuals can drown in fishing nets, be illegally shot by fishermen or die in oilspills. Many otters died in the massive shock waves generated by nuclear explosions when the Aleutians were used as a testing ground (see page 109). One sea otter cub is known to have been killed when hit by a boat propeller. This latter type of killing may seem trivial when compared with nuclear explosions, but it can be particularly common in prime fishing areas; some irresponsible boat owners intentionally speed through large rafts of resting otters. Commercial hunting may have ceased, but sea otters are still dying, indirectly but unnecessarily, at human hands.

5

Feeding Habits

Although sea otters congregate in large rafts, they also commute to favorite feeding grounds closer to shore. Females with cubs seek the solitude of these feeding territories and linger there longer. This home stretch of coast may measure several miles in length but extends less than .25 miles (.5 km) out to sea. In California female otters can utilize about 200 acres of coast, more if human disturbance is not a problem; males occupy territories about half that size. There is some degree of overlap between neighboring otters, but the animals usually succeed in finding some degree of privacy without undue intrusion from rivals.

Detailed studies of long-distance movements depend upon animals that are individually recognizable, either by the fixing of plastic tags on the flippers or by the use of radio transmitters. At first the tiny radios were attached by means of neck collars, but otters are slippery customers and were able to rid themselves easily of this high-tech apparatus. Researchers then fixed the radios to flippers but feared they might be hampering the otters. Recently there has been much more success by surgically implanting the devices in the otter's abdominal wall. This sounds like a drastic measure, but it is now a safe, routine operation, well justified by the results it produces. Nowadays, sea otters are at considerable risk from oil spills, so it is essential to know enough about the animal's behavior to predict how the population might respond to such a catastrophe. An animal's territory is actively defended from intruders, in the case of the sea otter for the duration of the breeding season only. A male sea otter holds a favored stretch of water to court estrous females, who themselves will defend only the immediate area around their cubs. A home range, on the other hand, encompasses the entire area frequented by an otter during the year, or even in its lifetime. Unlike territories, home ranges are not mutually exclusive and overlap extensively. The extent of each home range is influenced by the individual's age, sex, reproductive status and the season of the year.

On the whole females are more sedentary than males, although a few have been recorded traveling up to 30 miles (50 km). Females with young cubs range over several hundred square

Feeding Habits **67**

Sea otter asleep with paws covering its eyes

miles, gradually restricting their movements again as the cubs near independence.

Once separated from its mother, the cub may then embark on more extensive forays. One juvenile male in California covered no less than 116 miles (187 km), and the average distance achieved by seven of his peers was 48 miles (77 km). Juvenile females are less prone to quit their natal areas; those that do tend to travel less widely than young males. The speed with which such journeys are achieved can vary. One young Alaskan female traveled 25 miles (40 km) within three days of independence, while two males covered 50 miles (80 km) and 76 miles (123 km) respectively within the space of two weeks. A male in Prince William Sound clocked up 7 miles (11 km) in only two hours, and speeds of 3 miles (5 km) per hour may not be unusual.

After an initial wanderlust, a sea otter may then settle down. Its home range will include the breeding territory, the feeding or wintering areas and the travel corridors between the two. As already mentioned, some adult males occupy breeding territories all the year round, while others may travel widely, distances of 63 miles (100 km) being recorded in Prince William Sound, for example. Exactly why some individuals may undertake such journeys is not clear, but it is a fact that they represent only a small proportion of the population. In a sample of ninety-seven

68   Sea Otters

otters tagged in California, for instance, only six ventured more than 5 miles (8 km). One male undertook a journey 75 miles (121 km) to the south no fewer than six times (once in the space of only four days); each time he returned to the exact same kelp bed. Another moved 80 miles (129 km) north after being tagged, then, six weeks later, was seen 110 miles (177 km) to the south.

One male, tagged off Pacific Grove in mid-April 1981, enjoyed a brief but well-traveled existence thereafter. Known as Red 70, he spent that summer in a male group 35 miles (56 km) to the north. On October 7 he was seen at Monterey in hot pursuit of a female but two days later had resumed a bachelor lifestyle in a male group nearby. On November 9 he had rejoined the male group 35 miles to the north. By January 1982, he had taken up territory again at Monterey, associating with various females (some with cubs) until June. The last positive sighting of Red 70 was on April 14, 1983, and exactly one month later he was found shot in Moss Landing, presumably on another of his long journeys north.

Within their individual home ranges sea otters have fairly regular routines. They usually begin diving for food an hour after sunrise, and feeding and grooming activity reaches a peak between 6:00 and 8:00 A.M. Around midday comes a lull while the animals sleep or doze. Lying on their backs, perhaps with their paws covering their eyes, they often wrap a few thick strands of kelp around their bodies to serve as an anchor while they slumber; this prevents them drifting off and buffers the dozy creatures from rough seas. A group of otters sleeping near each other like this will drift to and fro in unison, like a team of laid-back synchronized swimmers. If no kelp is handy, the animals move further offshore to congregate in the safety of larger rafts. In northern latitudes with no humans to disturb them, they may even venture ashore to rest (see box, page 50).

Toward midafternoon a second bout of diving and grooming gets underway, reaching a peak at about 5:00 P.M. This is a busier period than the morning, with more than half of the animals in the group at any one time being engaged in some activity or other. Things become quieter again toward dusk. Discreet use of floodlights in Monterey Bay, California, revealed that a third bout of activity takes place around midnight, and, in fact, one-third of an otter's food may be procured at this time. Neither the tide nor nighttime seems to influence this cycle of behavior very much. Strong wind is more disruptive of the routine. In California the prevailing northwesterly winds blow strongest in the afternoons. The otters get little rest and tend to spend more of their afternoons feeding.

Radio transmitters reveal what otters are doing even under cover of darkness. The signals received by the researcher ashore are interrupted whenever the otter dives. Short, frequent interruptions indicate that the otter is swimming and diving, while a steady signal means the animal is resting. In Prince William Sound, Alaskan sea otters spend 40–50 percent of the day feeding. This increases to 70 percent in the wintertime, when the animal needs more food to keep warm, and food is harder to find. Adult males, solitary females and subadults of both sexes forage for about eleven hours each day, yearling otters for about an hour longer, and females with a cub feed for about thirteen hours. One female was timed foraging for 13.7 hours until its cub died, and it then reduced its activity to only 11.5 hours. A mother with a very young cub is reluctant to leave it alone at the surface while she dives and reduces her foraging to about 2 percent of the daylight hours; it is possible, however, that she may make up some of the deficiency under cover of darkness.

On a typical day a Monterey sea otter seems to spend about 24 percent of the daylight hours foraging, 5 percent interacting with other otters, 5 percent grooming, 5 percent swimming and no less than 62 percent resting. This behavior is similar to activity patterns of otters along parts of the Oregon coast and on the island of Attu in the Aleutians. Both these localities have only recently been colonized by sea otters, and food is still easy to come by. On the other hand, on Amchitka in the Aleutians, where the species has been long established and has now reached quite a high density, food is much harder won. In consequence, the animals there have to spend 50–60 percent of their day looking for it—the highest foraging rates yet recorded. It is tempting to argue that different environmental conditions prevail at these various localities, accounting for such disparity in feeding activity. Sea

Sea otter underwater

temperatures certainly differ between California and Amchitka, but both Attu and Amchitka are in the Aleutians, and conditions should be comparable.

Another investigation into the question was undertaken at two localities only 30 miles (50 km) apart in Prince William Sound. Here radio telemetry was used, so the results cannot be directly compared with the direct observation technique used above. In this case a "day" is twenty-four hours rather than the period of daylight. Nonetheless, it confirmed the idea that foraging rates are linked to availability of food, which in turn is influenced by the density of otters and the length of time they have been established in the area. Green Island otters (a long-established colony) spent 48 percent of each day feeding, while in Nelson Bay (where the species has only recently established) they spent only 37 percent of their day in this activity. The difference becomes even more marked when one considers that the Nelson Bay otters were feeding in deeper water, with stronger winds and currents, and had to commute a greater distance between their feeding and resting grounds. Had the conditions there been as amenable as Green Island, the Nelson Bay animals would probably have needed to spend even less time feeding. It seems that the Green Island otters had depleted their food supply to such an extent that they gained only 60 to 105 kilocalories in

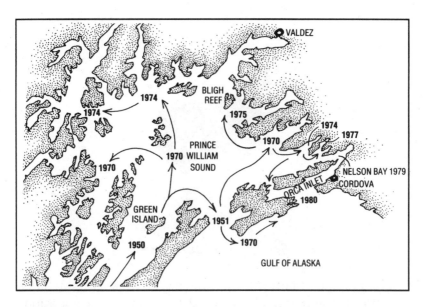

The spread of sea otters in Prince William Sound, Alaska, and the study areas of Green Island and Nelson Bay

half an hour's foraging. At Nelson Bay, however, large clams (offering a better calorific return) were still quite numerous and an otter could glean 1,000 kilocalories in the same time period.

Sea otters gather their food on or near the bottom, mostly within half a mile of the shore.They occasionally may forage farther out to sea, up to ten miles (16 km) but closer to shore they are usually over reefs where the water depth is not too great. One hundred feet (30 m) seems the normal depth limit, up to 200 feet (60 m) in calm weather or if the food supplies are rich enough to warrant the extra effort involved. Sea otters are probably capable of going even deeper, and one fisherman has recovered the skeleton of an adult male in a crab pot which was set at 350 feet (106 m).

The length of dives will vary according to the water depth. In shallow water they may be as brief as 15 seconds, but in 70 feet (23 m) of water they average between 50 and 80 seconds, with a maximum of 160 seconds. Females with a cub may stay underwater for about 50 seconds; in rough water they feed further offshore

Sea otter with beer can

with longer dives averaging 76 seconds. If alarmed or pursued a sea otter can remain submerged for even longer still. One female chased by a boat made thirteen dives ranging from 30 to 250 seconds (average 120) and even then showed little sign of exhaustion; at 205 seconds her last dive was one of the longest. It is unlikely that a sea otter can remain underwater for any longer than about 6 minutes.

Dive times can also vary according to the prey being sought and the length of time needed to procure it. With clumps of mussels that are relatively easily detached, Monterey sea otters surface after thirty seconds or so. With other food items, particularly if the dive has been unsuccessful, the animal emerges after fifty-five seconds.

The diet of sea otters is varied. It includes urchins, mussels, abalones, limpets, scallops, annelid worms, crabs, fish, fish eggs and octopuses. The latter sometimes seek refuge in empty beer and cola cans lying on the seabed, but recently some resourceful otters have been seen tearing open the aluminum cans with their strong teeth to get at the little delicacy inside. About half such cans contain octopuses—never more than one per can. In fifteen minutes one otter recovered eight cans from the seabed, taking no more than a minute to rip open each one and winning for itself five small octopuses.

This may be an appropriate juncture at which to describe the teeth of a sea otter. An adult sea otter has thirty-two teeth. The

Feeding Habits **73**

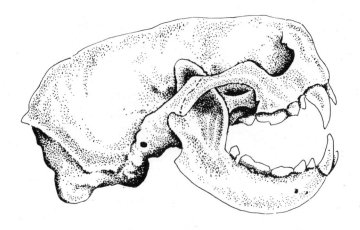

Sea otter skull

incisors are spade-shaped and protrude slightly to facilitate the scooping out of shellfish. There are three pairs of incisors on the upper jaw but only two pairs on the lower (among carnivores a feature unique to sea otters and seals). The large canines are rounded, having no sharp point or sharp cutting edge. In fact, they are often worn or broken in older animals, because they are used to pry open the valves of oysters and other bivalve mollusks—as well as aluminum beer cans! The powerful cheek teeth are flattened and rounded for crushing invertebrates, whereas in most other carnivores they are adapted for shearing and cutting flesh. An adult sea otter has three pairs of premolars top and bottom, with two pairs of molars on the lower jaw and one pair on the upper.

A newborn cub has ten teeth already erupted—two upper incisors, four canines and four lower premolars. Other deciduous teeth (which will later be shed) appear within the first two or three months, and the adult set of teeth erupts by the end of the first year.

By constant crushing of hard-shelled mollusks and urchins that are often covered in sand, sea otters' teeth can become very worn. In old animals this can result in their starving to death. Captive otters fed on a diet of soft foods suffer much less tooth wear.

74   Sea Otters

The resourceful sea otter is the only mammal, other than primates, to employ tools in finding food. As it lies on its back in the water, an otter will often place a stone on its chest to use as an anvil. It then bangs a mussel against the stone until the shell cracks. This behavior was first recorded in 1939 and has since attracted much interest from animal behaviorists. Californian mussels are about 2 inches (5 cm) long. Holding a mussel in its front paws, the otter will bring the shell down on the stone with an audible click. The first bang is usually a tentative one, as though the otter is aligning the shell on the anvil. There then follow up to twenty-two blows—one every two seconds; the animal then tests the shell by biting it. If it is still undamaged the whole procedure is repeated. On average six bouts of hammering are required to break open a mussel shell, about thirty-five blows in all. One particularly hard shell required fifteen bouts and eighty-eight blows. One otter feeding on mussels for eighty-six minutes dived fifty-four times and at the surface delivered no less than 2,237 blows.

The stones that are chosen as anvils are usually quite smooth, about 6 inches (15 cm) in diameter and weigh about half a pound (.2 kg). Of thirty-six examined closely, about a third were relatively flat, the remainder being more irregular in shape. Occasionally, the same one may be retained for several dives. In one series of observations, the same stone was kept for twelve dives; in another, six different stones were used to deal with forty-four mussels. Sometimes a new stone is used for each item. Favored stones are held under the armpit while diving. On one occasion an otter was seen to surface with a boulder reckoned almost 8 pounds (3.5 kg), but having no food to bang on it, the otter dropped this colossus immediately. Otters have even been seen pounding their chests without having either a stone or a mussel.

In parts of Alaska, especially in winter, individuals may venture ashore to deal with prey, but this is distinctly unusual. Breaking mussels with a stone is rare in Alaska, and it has never been recorded on the Commander Islands. In the sheltered bays and fjords of Alaska where the sea otters feed, the species of mussel *Mytilus edulis* thrives. This mussel has a thinner shell that

Feeding Habits 75

is easily crushed or pried open. *Mytilus californianus* occurs on more exposed shores and requires a thicker shell to withstand the wave action. In California the otter requires this ingenious means to exploit these bigger, hard-shelled mussels. Nonetheless, the otters from northern climes seem to possess the necessary skills. Susie, an Alaskan captive in Seattle Zoo, was seen to employ the technique when presented with mussels too large to be merely crushed in the jaws, her normal means of handling such prey. In fact she became quite attached to her stone and never let it out of her sight. Ultimately it had to be taken away from her when she started using it to smash the concrete sides of her pool. But this apparent act of vandalism was merely mimicking a technique used to knock abalones off rocks.

Hammering skills begin to be acquired at an early age. In California cubs begin to make crude chest-slapping movements with the forepaws at about five weeks. One seven-week-old cub was watched hitting an abalone shell on its chest with empty paws. At nine and a half weeks it was pounding and rubbing two pieces of shell together and would dive several times in succession holding a stone. It was seen to pound a kelp crab against its chest at fourteen weeks and at nineteen and a half weeks at last used a stone successfully to open a shell. By the time they are five or six months old sea otter cubs seem well able to handle and consume prey using either their teeth or a stone. Other prey like abalones are more difficult to cope with, so mussels, particularly the small ones which can be swallowed whole or crushed easily, are a useful resort for young inexperienced otters. Although they have a poorer nutritional value and calorific content, mussel beds are often frequented by a mother and her cub so that the youngster can begin its career on "easy meat." Mussel beds are also resorted to by adult otters when their offshore feeding grounds are inaccessible in stormy weather.

In California 40 percent of the sea otter's diet might be mussels, 33 percent sea urchins, 15 percent crabs and 9 percent abalones. Small urchins are easily crushed in the teeth, larger ones bitten apart to expose the soft insides. Spawning urchins are a particularly favorite and nutritious food. It takes an otter about thirty-eight seconds to deal with an urchin, compared with fifty

Sea otter with octopus

seconds or more when hammering a mussel. With a crab, the otter needs only to bite off one leg before beginning to tear the rest apart. This grisly operation may last several minutes, and at first the poor crab may run round and round the otter's chest trying to escape its tormentor's clutches. Octopuses also remain active for some minutes while being eaten, wrapping sticky tentacles round the otter's head in a vain attempt to pull free.

Abalones have a single convex shell which clings to a rock, limpetlike, with a strong, muscular foot. They occur singly or in small groups under rock ledges near the bottom. Red abalones can be up to 12 inches (30 cm) across, the black species rarely exceeding 4 inches (10 cm). The sea otter uses a rock to dislodge them—another, though less novel, example of tool use. Diving otters have been watched carrying stones in their forepaws. Once they locate an abalone, they hammer at it with very short but powerful arm movements from the chest. An extra bone in the wrist of the sea otter (not found in any other mammal) gives additional leverage for pulling obstinate abalones from rocks. Skin divers have been attracted to a busy sea otter by the pounding sounds of its rock tool penetrating through the water. Two interested human spectators, swimming about 30 feet (10 m) beneath the surface, were harassed by one irritable (or just

Feeding Habits **77**

inquisitive) otter—they were fumbled and frisked by the animal before it finally bit the end of a snorkel! The otter then surfaced for some air before returning to pick up a flattish granite stone weighing nearly 2 pounds (1 kg). Using this stone, it hammered at a 5-inch (12 cm) abalone shell on a rock ledge nearby. The otter surfaced for air again before resuming its task, occasionally pausing to pull at the shell. It surfaced yet again, leaving the rock behind this time, but retrieved it before finally dislodging its quarry, the shell intact.

ABALONE ATTACKS UNDERWATER

The sea otter is the only sea mammal to use tools. The whacking sound made by the animal smashing shellfish on its rock anvil would alert the old Californian otter hunters. Nowadays, the hammering of abalones on the seabed incurs the wrath of commercial shellfishermen.

Two cameramen from California once decided to film the sea otter's underwater behavior. They gathered up some abalones and transferred them to areas suitable for filming. The otters took advantage of the handouts but too quickly for the mollusks to attach themselves, so filming the hammering operation proved impossible. So the camera team first allowed some abalones to cling to a large boulder within the confines of a sack before the otters were given access. The first otter to appear on the set tentatively tugged at the shells, then scooped up the boulder, complete with abalones, and took it to the surface for treatment. Foiled once more, the patient camera crew finally offered a massive rock with abalones attached. An otter dived down to wiggle its whiskers enthusiastically over the rock, gave a few tugs, then set about the tasty offerings with a rock hammer. The camera rolled. The star unkindly rejected all the meager implements scattered nearby by the humans, preferring one of its own choosing, 1 foot (30 cm) long, 6 inches (15 cm) broad and 3 inches (8 cm) thick. Not surprisingly, only one whack was needed to dislodge the first abalone—which was catapulted straight into the eager hands of another otter looking on. Our hero was not to be outdone, however, and pursued the thief to the surface and retrieved his hardwon prize.

The processed film and other underwater observations showed that a side attack on an abalone is the most effective, often requiring only a single blow. Pounding straight down with a rock merely smashes the shell without detaching it. Best of all, if it proved possible, was an upward sweep with the rock to attack the under edge of a protruding abalone. One totally inexperienced otter has been seen trying to bite off an abalone and then, totally frustrated, picking up a rock and pounding his chest with it!

Gathering abalones requires several dives of long duration and a further ten minutes or more to deal with them at the surface. The large, soft body is untidily scooped out of the shell in portions. While thus engaged the otter rolls in the water several times, sweeping off waste and broken bits of shell to keep its fur clean. Gulls frequently wait nearby for such scraps, and they may congregate patiently in twos and threes waiting for a feeding otter to surface. Skin divers have also noted parties of a dozen or more fish waiting below a feeding otter to feed on the "fallout" of mussel scraps, becoming especially excited whenever the otter rolls to wash debris off its chest.

With some 25 ounces (700 g) of flesh, one abalone certainly seems worth the time and effort involved. In contrast red urchins provide only 8 ounces (230 g), purple urchins only .75 ounces (22 g) and mussels a mere .33 ounces (10 g). Three abalones, with a crab for dessert, could provide a complete day's requirement for a hungry otter. In the space of nearly three hours one glutton was observed to eat eighteen gaper clams, fifteen crabs, two moon snails, one black abalone, one octopus and eight other items that the observer could not identify. But such variety in taste appears to be unusual. Otters observed in California seem to specialize in a few prey species only, often differing entirely

Feeding Habits **79**

Eating fish

from their neighbors along the same stretch of coast. While feeding on abalones, for instance, one animal will ignore urchins or mussels that are the staple of the otter next door. Others excavate soft sand to find burrowing shellfish or mudworms. In such activities the sense of touch is vital in locating prey through the murky clouds of silt. At Amchitka in Alaska, the resident otters form two distinct groups. Some feed mostly on invertebrates, and indeed their bones become stained with the purple pigment from their urchin prey. Others eat mostly fish—a habit also well developed in the Kurile Islands of Russia. However, sea otters are not particularly good fishermen, having to catch fish in their paws and surface with their slippery prey clasped precariously to their chests. Once at the surface the otters can transfer the fish to their jaws. If a fish or octopus is large, the otter may doze off with its unfinished meal clutched to its chest until ready to tackle a second helping.

Sea otters sometimes catch birds, but this is unusual and they may not even find the flesh particularly palatable. A fulmar or shearwater, a cormorant, a teal and a captive Emperor goose have all been recorded falling victim to Alaskan otters. The habit may be slightly more common in California, where sea otters have been seen eating two western grebes, two freshly dead cormorants and a gull. A surf scoter harassed by an otter managed to escape, whereas, in the same area, two great northern diver carcasses looked as though they might have been devoured by otters. All these instances may have been the activities of only a few individual sea otters that were particularly adept at bird catching. On the other hand, they may have been experiencing difficulty in catching other prey.

Sea otters have the ability to hoard food items in loose flaps of skin under each foreleg; these flaps extend out to the chest to form a convenient pouch. Both paws may be used to lift items, but only the right one is used to push them into the pouch—under the left forearm. The left paw is used only if the animal is trying to clutch more food than it can normally cope with. Similarly, food is retrieved from the pouch only by the right paw. Lefthanded otters seem not to exist! An otter was seen to surface from a dive with half a dozen urchins and three large oysters stowed under its arm; its cub then greedily snatched the largest urchin and crushed it in its paws to scoop out the rich egg masses inside. Captive otters have been seen storing their own rations under one arm while they tried to steal more food from one another! One captive otter succeeded in stuffing no fewer than eighteen clams, each 1.5 inches (4 cm) in diameter, into its pouches; however, the addition of a nineteenth was the last straw, causing the hoard to spill out. Even clutching eight clams the otter was able to walk with ease on three legs. The species can be tenacious with a particularly prized morsel. One individual was pursued—by an equally determined biologist—for no less than two hours. As soon as it knew it was safe, the animal smugly retrieved a prickly sea urchin from under its left arm and resumed its meal!

6

Predation and Ecological Impact

Sea otters are actively mobile predators with particularly healthy appetites. They are all the more efficient at their job because of the sluggish or stationary lifestyle of their prey. Indeed, the only way such things as abalones or urchins can escape the otter's grasp is by taking refuge in rock crevices. Shellfish that are below an optimum size tend to be ignored, as do those that live in water too deep for the otter to work effectively.

Sea otters have the capability of radically altering the make up of animal and plant communities in coastal waters. The details of this complex ecological relationship were first identified in Alaska. By a quirk of the sea otters' unhappy history, the Near Islands in the Aleutians lost their otter population last century. The Rat Islands farther to the east, however, retained a small population that multiplied and, for several decades, has maintained a high density. The sea gap to the Near Islands, despite the name, is 250 miles (400 km) wide, and none of the Rat Island otters has yet managed to negotiate this inhospitable channel. Thus, the two archipelagos, with their similar environmental conditions, provide neat laboratories in which to investigate inshore ecosystems with and without otters.

Amchitka, the largest of the ten Rat Islands, reflects a situation that probably prevailed before man ever set foot on the island. It is surrounded just offshore by dense beds—often termed *forests*—of marine algae, particularly several species of kelp such as *Macrocystis* and *Nereocystis*. Together with a dense understory of shorter red and brown seaweeds, this algal mass buffers the shoreline from the worst effects of storms and permits the accumulation of silt, in which barnacles, mussels, clams and other sessile invertebrates find it difficult to survive. You will recall that it is around Amchitka that sea otters occur in good numbers. They have eaten out the large sea urchins, which are voracious grazers of seaweeds, so that the small urchins that remain have little effect on the kelp. Thus, the otters have had to turn to fish, which shelter in the kelp fronds, and any other invertebrates they can find.

Traveling to the Near Islands, the difference is dramatic even to the casual observer on the shore. There are no sea otters to be seen, and no tangle of kelp fronds protrudes through the

Predation and Ecological Impact **85**

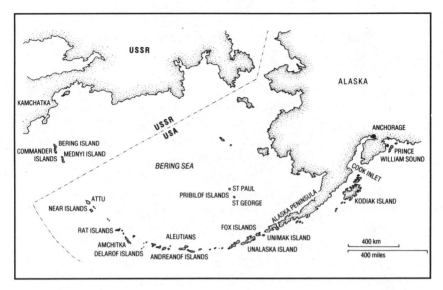

The Aleutian and Commander islands in the Bering Sea

water at low tide. Donning a wet suit and aqualung, the observer will discover that the seafloor just offshore is virtually devoid of seaweed, but sea urchins are everywhere, including many large ones. There are extensive mussel beds and dense populations of barnacles, colonial tubeworms, starfish and octopuses. Can the lack of sea otters really cause such a difference?

Some scientists would answer yes. Sea otters eat urchins and effectively control their numbers. Urchins graze voraciously on seaweed, and where they have been depleted by otters, various algae, notably kelp, can thrive to form dense forests. Remove the otters and the urchins take over, virtually eliminating the kelp beds. This keystone role accorded to the otters even extends beyond algae and invertebrates to affect higher animals. Fish find refuge in the kelp forest and in turn attract common seals and bald eagles, species rarely seen around the Near Islands but sighted frequently on the Rat group.

In recent years, a small population of sea otters has safely negotiated the sea gap to become established near Chichagof Harbor on Attu, the largest of the Near Islands. It will be an acid test of the keystone predator hypothesis if Attu's urchin barrens turn into the kelp forests common around Amchitka. So far all that has happened is that the larger urchins have been devoured, leaving the smaller ones (unattractive to the otters) to enjoy a better survival rate and reach higher densities. A significant increase in kelp has yet to be noted, but it may only become apparent once the otters have completely encircled the island of Attu and competition for food increases. On another of the Aleutians, Adak Island, sea urchins were reported as abundant and obvious until the sea otters began to reestablish; now there are few urchins to be found.

But it may have been, for some reason the scientists have yet to identify, that there never were large urchins to be found on

Diving for urchins . . .

Predation and Ecological Impact 87

. . . and eating one

the island of Amchitka. However, in deep water, beyond the range of sea otters, they are common. Furthermore, excavations of ancient kitchen middens on the island have revealed that the Aleuts used to gather them to eat. Indeed these prehistoric rubbish dumps have given some interesting insights into the sea otter/urchin/kelp relationship and the effect of early human hunters on the environment.

The Aleuts arrived in the western Aleutian Islands about twenty-five hundred years ago. They lived by hunting animals such as seals, sea otters and fish and by gathering sea creatures along the beach—shrimps, shellfish, urchins, etc. Thus, the empty shells and bones, discarded on the campsite middens, are the best indication we have of what the local nearshore communities looked like in prehistoric times. Of course, softbodied creatures are not preserved at all, and the easily decomposed bones of salmon and lumpsucker so favored by modern Aleuts will be underrepresented in the midden samples. But such biases prevail at every level of the midden and all we seek to do is compare the frequency of the shellfish in the various zones. In most recent times, the Aleuts were discarding bones of fish, seals and otters rather than shellfish. Radiocarbon methods date these deposits as only a few centuries old. Below this, about a thousand years ago, remains of these vertebrate animals are scarce but sea urchins and limpets are common. At the very bottom, represent-

88   Sea Otters

ing the period when Aleuts first colonized the island, the situation reverses back to fish, seals and otters, with shellfish being ignored.

These patterns may sound familiar. It seems likely that the first Aleut colonists found vertebrate prey abundant, and no doubt kelp forests flourished offshore. Once they had hunted out these creatures—notably, from our point of view, otters—the urchins and mollusks became abundant and formed an alternative, if less favored, diet. The Aleuts had to seek larger prey further afield, which allowed the sea otters to recover their numbers somewhat. The urchins became scarce again, the kelp came back and so did the fish and the seals; thus, the cycle could begin once more.

This is of course a gross oversimplification, not only of the excavation results but of the deductions made from them. Nonetheless, it does underline the keystone role apparently played by the sea otter in nearshore communities, disrupted only when man appeared on the scene. His early depredations, remember, would have been local; only modern man has had the power to decimate the sea otter on a worldwide scale.

What of the situation farther south? Do sea otters play the same role along the Californian coast? In the 1930s, they were exceedingly scarce, being confined to only one locality—Big Sur south of Carmel. From here they eventually spread both north and south, to occupy some 200 miles (320 km) of coast from Año Nuevo to Morro Bay. Concurrent with this recent expansion in range, there seems to have been a spread in kelp; we know this because the U.S. Department of Agriculture had mapped out this scarce resource earlier this century.

But can we be sure that the sea otters were responsible for the return of the kelp? As in Alaska, one can compare areas before and after the arrival of the otters. In the 1950s, for example, Monterey Bay had high densities of urchins; but within ten years of the sea otters' arrival, kelp had taken over. The fine detail of this effect may soon be elucidated at San Nicolas Island, where the seabed was surveyed in anticipation of the reintroduction of otters (a program that will be described in Chapter 7).

The otter/urchin/kelp effect can even be simulated artificially. In both California and Alaska, urchins have been persis-

Predation and Ecological Impact **89**

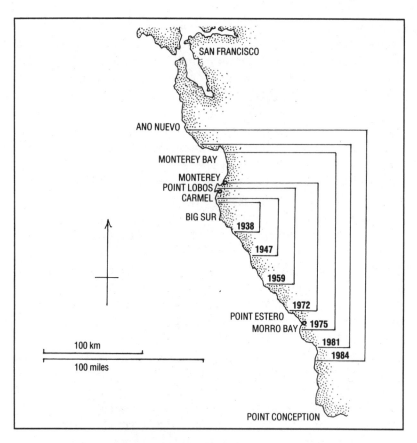

The expansion of sea otters in California

tently removed by skin divers from seabed plots, thereby creating, as expected, new kelp forests. It is impossible to do the reverse experiment, however, namely removing sea otters to see if urchin barrens result; ethical and legal considerations, not to mention the conservationists, just would not allow it!

Some scientists still remain skeptical. They argue that kelp forests and urchin barrens are merely two extremes, and the commonly occurring state lies somewhere in between. Among over two hundred study plots examined along the Californian coast, only nineteen could be classed as true urchin barrens. Furthermore, they point out that similar habitats can be created under natural conditions, without urchins, when unusually severe storms clear away much of the kelp. Conversely, in the absence of otters, large urchin populations can be decimated by rough seas, by disease or by pollution from sewage outfalls, resulting in a proliferation of kelp. Even with otters present, the herbivorous urchins can often find adequate refuge in particularly rocky substrata and in areas where water turbulence inhibits the establishment of kelp.

One final factor seems never before to have been considered. Steller's sea cows were huge and voracious browsers of the giant kelp. These once numerous herbivores formerly shared the entire range of the sea otter (including, no doubt, California), although by the time western man appeared on the scene, the animals were restricted to only one locality, the Commander Islands. It cannot be ignored that the now extinct sea cow would have exerted a powerful impact on the kelp beds, a role that the humble sea urchin has now had to assume. Perhaps the situation we witness today is an attempt by the kelp ecosystem to restore an ecological balance in the absence of the ravenous sea cow.

A FOREST OF SEAWEED

The giant kelp of the North Pacific is a remarkable plant by any standards. It flourishes in offshore coastal waters, withstanding quite rough, stormy seas. Each plant clings tenaciously to the rock floor with a "holdfast," and it is from this that the frond develops. It grows at an astonishing rate of 2 feet (.6 m) a day, to reach a total length of some 230 feet (70 m). After four or five months of hectic growth, the mature strands then die. At once new fronds sprout, so that a giant kelp plant (indeed, the whole forest) regenerates itself completely about twice a year.

Algin is the unusual chemical from which kelp derives its remarkable resistance to wave action. It also has many other properties which are useful to man. As an emulsifier, for instance, it binds oily and watery fluids together and proves

Predation and Ecological Impact **91**

essential in the production of paints, cosmetics and pharmaceuticals; it is added to salad dressings, ice cream, cake icing, toothpastes and seventy other diverse products, being especially important in the manufacturing of paper and textiles.

In California alone, there are over 100 square miles of kelp forest. Huge seagoing lawnmowers cut over 5 tons a day, with state regulations limiting commercial harvesting to a depth of just over 3 feet (1 m) below the surface. Sea otters come to no harm since the boats are so noisy and move so slowly. Between 1966 and 1976 some 290 million pounds (133 million kg) was being harvested each year in California, worth about $20 million. Some economists would venture to suggest that kelp contributes more to American coffers than does the threatened luxury market for shellfish. But it is strange that such a vast industry should feel threatened by the apparently insignificant sea urchin. This voracious herbivore attacks the lower parts of the kelp plant, near the holdfast, and the dismembered frond floats away to die. The kelp companies spend considerable sums of money in controlling sea urchins and, not surprisingly, consider the sea otter to be quite a powerful ally.

Kelp forests support a wealth of other marine life—crabs, lobsters, abalone, rock scallops and top snails, in addition to myriads of fish such as kelp bass, perch, croakers and rock fish. These of course attract considerable interest from recreational fishermen and skin divers, providing an additional economic spinoff from the kelp beds.

Most of us will never experience what it is like to swim through this marine jungle. However, Monterey Aquarium has created a complete kelp forest in a gigantic tank, 30 feet (10 m) tall and containing 335,000 gallons of sea water. Thus, everyone can enjoy this impressive undersea spectacle through special, thick acrylic windows—without ever getting wet feet!

Whatever the theoreticians say, the fact remains that the sea otter does have a considerable impact on the nearshore invertebrate fauna, which can in turn affect the abundance of marine algae. The extensive urchin barrens that resulted from the

92 Sea Otters

exploitation of otters by the fur trade last century provided ideal conditions for shellfish. The resulting rich fisheries are now important commercially and for sporting purposes. Following their legal protection in 1911 and the resultant increase in numbers, sea otters also came to appreciate this bonanza in shellfish. So it is not surprising that they came into conflict with the shellfisherman.

The problem first arose with the abalone fishery in central California. Abalones had been gathered as food by man for thousands of years, but only in this century did divers begin to exploit them to any great extent. After the Second World War, with the introduction of wet suits, the fishery expanded. The appetite of Japan for seafoods created an industry that handles some 1.5 million pounds (700,000 kg) of abalones from California alone; a further 570,000 pounds (260,000 kg) come from more northerly fishing grounds. When red and pink abalones became scarce, attention turned to the less tasty blues, greens and whites. Now all colors are declining, both in California and elsewhere. The catch of a British Columbia diver, for instance, may now amount to less than 300 pounds (137 kg) a day, compared with 450 pounds (205 kg) a few years ago. Following a peak year in Alaska in 1979, a closed season has now had to be introduced and quotas imposed.

Declines in California are blamed on the sea otter. Certainly the density of red abalones at Point Estero, for example, declined from 0.24 per square foot to 0.03 following the arrival of sea otters. But, with few otters in British Columbia as yet and none in Mexico, abalones have still become scarce. This might suggest that man himself is involved, taking more abalones than stocks can withstand. And it is not just the commercial fisherman who is responsible; information is still poor, but recreational fishing is reckoned to account for as much, if not more, than the big operators; furthermore, recreational fishing is often subject to less stringent legal regulations and monitoring.

While both fishermen and sea otters undoubtedly can hasten the demise of certain abalone fisheries, the mollusk itself has certain built-in characteristics that make it especially susceptible to overfishing. Abalones have infrequent bouts of spawning. Initially, both fisherman and otter concentrate their efforts on the

Predation and Ecological Impact **93**

old individuals whose numbers have taken a long time to accumulate. Since abalones are long lived and slow growing, the population will be slow to recover from this initial impact.

In Alaska, conflicts between man and otter have the potential of attaining crisis proportions because the shellfisheries are so important to the local economy and because sea otters are so numerous. Dungeness crabs are one important shellfish resource. The best fishing grounds around Orca Inlet in Prince William Sound were largely destroyed by the tectonic uplift and tidal waves of the 1964 earthquake. The crab population slowly recovered, but in 1980, coinciding with the arrival of large numbers of sea otters, the catches began to decline again. A similar situation was observed nearby in Nelson Bay and immediately all local crab fishing was stopped. Fears for stocks were then expressed as otters began to recolonize other fishing grounds. However, a successful crab industry has been maintained in the Gulf of Alaska, where sea otters have existed for over forty years. Indeed the whole commercial enterprise for Dungeness crabs was initiated in San Francisco last century; catches there soon began to decline—*in the complete absence of any sea otters.* In fact, annual crab populations along the whole North American coast seem influenced by a variety of factors—changing oceanic condition, rising sea temperatures, pollution, parasites, even obscure fluctuations apparently cycling in tandem with sunspots.

Razor clams are another important species, and in 1917 over 4.4 million pounds (2 million kg) were landed in Alaska; indeed, the town of Cordova in Prince William Sound was known as the "razor clam capital of the world." Recently, catches have declined—by no less than 80 percent following the 1964 earthquake. But there has also been damage from competition rival clam fisheries in the Atlantic and from occasional outbreaks of paralytic shellfish poisoning. Of course, the sea otters are also blamed. In fact, the otters only recolonized the principal beds in Prince William Sound in the late 1970s, when the clams were already scarce. Admittedly, they could be one of the factors now keeping harvestable clam densities at low levels. Over 90 percent of the razor clam catch now goes as bait for the Dungeness crab fishery.

94   Sea Otters

Kelp forest in Monterey aquarium

Predation and Ecological Impact **95**

Elsewhere in Alaska are other substantial commercial shellfisheries that might be affected by sea otters. But in Prince William Sound at least, the confrontation between fisherman and otter has now become academic, since the livelihood of both has been severely damaged by the recent catastrophic oil spill (see Chapter 8).

Similar scenarios are to be found much further south in California. Pismo clams are much sought-after mollusks occurring on surf-swept sand beaches off southern California and Mexico, where harvesting began about 1916. Catches peaked only two years later at over 650,000 pounds (300,000 kg) and have declined ever since—all this in the absence of sea otters. The commercial fishery closed soon after the war, but harvesting pismo clams is still a popular sport. No clams under 4 inches (10 cm) across can be taken. However, improper digging by divers is damaging stocks of the smaller clams, as is driving motor vehicles over the clam beaches at low tide. Recruitment of young mollusks into the population is often sporadic and poor. Sea otters, which moved back into the area in the 1970s, are being blamed for the lack of pismos, but even in the presence of the otters, recruitment of young clams should still have been possible, since otters ignore those less than 3 inches (7 cm) across, which are still capable of spawning. Furthermore, new clam beaches are colonized first by large groups of male sea otters, who do the initial damage. They usually move on, leaving the area to territorial males, breeding females and their cubs, all of which will have much less impact on the pismo beds. This has yet to happen but should give irate clam divers some crumbs of comfort for the future.

Smaller fisheries, such as rock crabs, butter clams and mussels, have all survived the presence of otters. Clearly, abalones and urchins are the hardest hit, especially where the sea floor provides few refuges in rock crevices. Most shellfish appear to suffer some degree of overfishing by man and are unable to sustain the initially large harvests—regardless of otter predation. Abnormally high market prices can prolong a profitable fishery long after the stock has been severely depleted. While reproduction (i.e., production of eggs) is always massive in mollusks, it is the number of larvae which make it back into the population each year as adults (what we call *recruitment*) that is crucial; together with subsequent growth rates recruitment can vary from place to place, even for the same species, and can be episodic with few breeding seasons proving really productive. Most species have to withstand pressure from both commercial *and* sporting interests, as discussed earlier. Shellfish beds are also susceptible to natural disasters such as the Alaskan earthquake and unnatural ones like the *Exxon Valdez* oil spill. They are also vulnerable to market demand; health scares often occur when shellfish begin to accumulate unusually high doses of toxins and environmental pollutants.

It is ironic that most of these fisheries became commercially viable in the first place because the sea otter had been hounded to the verge of extinction. We have seen how the presence of otters encourages the proliferation of kelp. This is a valuable economic resource in its own right, at first to be milled and dried as livestock feed but later of immense importance in the chemical industry. The kelp industry dislikes sea urchins and one company employs fifteen skin divers to destroy these little echinoderms; other control methods include the application of large quantities of poisonous quicklime to the seabed. Sea otters perform the same function for nothing!

The otters themselves can be an asset. For example, gift shops, galleries and many other retail outlets in Monterey stock many sea otter items—postcards, prints, T-shirts, puppets and soft toys, assorted trinkets and souvenirs, sculptures and paintings—priced from a few cents to hundreds of dollars. There are sets of china decorated with sea otters, a perfume (called The Otter's Secret) and even sea otter baby diapers! Furthermore, Monterey Public Library has chosen as its logo Monte, the literate sea otter. Tripper boats operate out of Monterey harbor specifically to show off the local sea otters to tourists. Sea otter watching is also a popular pastime in Alaska and contributes to local coffers not insubstantially. With a little more effort by the tourist agencies, the revenue could compensate for declining economic returns from shellfisheries.

So one's attitude toward sea otters is dependent upon whether one is a shellfisherman, a harvester of kelp, a tourist, a

Predation and Ecological Impact **97**

Diver destroying sea urchins

conservationist or just a member of the public. Over five thousand such people (from scientists to skin divers) subscribe to Friends of the Sea Otter—a conservation organization based in California (with its own shop in Carmel) whose international membership has campaigned on behalf of the species for twenty years. Many more people—the silent majority—may never see wild sea otters but derive intense enjoyment from watching film of them on TV; they are merely content in the knowledge that this endearing animal is once again swimming around its age-old haunts.

7
Captive Rearing and Relocation Efforts

ea otters can be confiding creatures, but when they first encountered the white man, they quickly learned their mistake. Only now are some beginning to show trust again. At the oil terminal of Valdez, in Prince William Sound, Alaska, one tame individual, affectionately known as Oscar, has lived these past five years among the moored fishing boats, cashing in on his charms to win scraps from locals and tourists alike. (Oscar, by the way, avoided the recent oil spill and now begs food beside the pens of the recuperating victims.) Since the late 1960s other wild otters have learned to exploit their instant appeal in Monterey Bay, California, where they too have become popular tourist attractions. Indeed, this is probably the best place to view wild otters at reasonably close quarters. Elsewhere, the animals can be more shy and, because of the nature of their rugged coastal haunts, even elusive.

Opportunities do exist to watch otters at closer quarters—but only animals held within the confines of a cage. Several North American and Japanese institutions keep sea otters. The first to be exhibited were transported from Alaska to the Seattle Zoo in February 1954; they were then transferred to Washington, D.C., but died soon afterward. On October 10, 1955, an otter named Susie came to Seattle Zoo and lived there for six years in a freshwater enclosure. Of eighteen more otters transported by

Sea otter in Monterey Harbor

Captive Rearing and Relocation Efforts **101**

air from Amchitka to Seattle, only one survived any length of time—a popular male called Gus. The new Seattle Aquarium obtained three adults in 1976 and a male the following year; it still exhibits sea otters. Point Defiance Zoo in Tacoma, Washington, received its first captives in 1965, and one has lived thirteen years. In 1969, the Vancouver Aquarium in British Columbia obtained its first sea otter, which was joined by two females in July 1972. The original male recently died at the ripe old age of nineteen. San Diego has exhibited sea otters since 1972, all of them from California.

The Monterey Aquarium has chosen to concentrate its efforts toward rehabilitating sick or injured sea otters. About fifty have been cared for since 1984, and many juveniles and adults have been successfully returned to the wild. Orphaned cubs are a different ball game altogether, and the aquarium has pioneered special techniques for handling them. It has developed a recipe to substitute for mother's milk. Older cubs receive a seafood milkshake, carefully blended from clam meat, squid, cod-liver oil, dextrose, minerals and vitamins. The little orphans seem to relish this concoction until they graduate to solid foods. Since a sea otter cub would ordinarily spend three-quarters of its early life sitting on the rolling and pitching chest of its mother, aquarium staff find a water bed to be a great substitute! The cubs become easily bored, however, so have to be given plastic toys to amuse them. In addition to such play, the youngsters also need constant handling, petting and grooming by their human foster mothers. The keepers likened their little charges to human babies—except that they need a lot more attention!

SEA OTTER ANTICS IN CAPTIVITY

After a few days of confinement sea otters usually become quite tame, some readily accepting food from the outset. Pieces of fish tossed at otters in the water are either caught in the paws or fielded against the chest. More aggressive individuals soon learn to come ashore to be first in the

102   Sea Otters

line and to accept food offered by the keeper—graciously avoiding the hand that feeds them! The prize is then tucked into the left armpit as the otter, on three legs, hobbles back to the water to eat. One particularly greedy female took to robbing her cage mates. Although the keeper tried to fend her off with a long pole, she soon learned to avoid his attentions by diving beneath her unsuspecting otter victim. Extending only one paw above the surface, she could safely snatch the food from its chest.

Not being especially adapted to a fish diet and lacking the shearing powers of the back teeth of other carnivores, sea otters can only tear off bite-sized chunks with their canines and incisors before masticating the flesh between the flattened molars (as they would do with shellfish). The head, larger bones and viscera of the fish are discarded. Fish and squid are popular convenience food to give captive otters, being easy to obtain and reasonably cheap, but the otters relish octopuses and mollusks. Captive otters have also been seen sampling a slice of white bread, a marshmallow and some peanuts, although the latter passed through the gut undigested.

On one occasion a rat was seen to approach a captive sea otter that was lying on its back grooming, close to the edge of its pool. After sniffing the otter's flank, the rat then suddenly leaped aboard! With its paw the otter deftly cuffed the rat from its chest, sending it flying about a yard (1 m). Stowaways are definitely not allowed on board!

It all began on February 19, 1983, with an ailing adult female found on a Santa Cruz beach. Diagnosed to have a twisted intestine, the otter was operated upon immediately. The next day, she was sitting up in her pen, eating a hearty breakfast. Over the next two weeks she gained 9 pounds (4 kg) and could be released back into the sea on March 5. Three weeks later a man jogging along Monterey Beach almost trod on an abandoned cub, partially buried in the sand. It was less than a week old and weighed just over 3 pounds (1 kg). The aquarium staff fed it from a bottle every hour and a half (day and night). At four months of age, it weighed a healthier 12 pounds (5 kg), but sadly died six months later.

Captive Rearing and Relocation Efforts **103**

Two female cubs—called Goldie and Hailey—as well as the cub named Milkdud were orphaned in 1984. After being successfully reared by the staff (and no fewer than fifty-six enthusiastic volunteers), they are now a popular exhibit at the aquarium. A fourth otter, a male called Roscoe, was found abandoned in March 1986, at only two weeks of age. As he grew older, he was taken by his human foster mother for regular swims in one of the aquarium's tidal tanks and taught to search for food under stones. In February 1987, at an age of eight months—by which time he should have been independent—he was released into the sea but became highly stressed by the unfamiliar surroundings. Six days later, and without having fed at all, he was encountered approaching humans on the beach in a desperate bid for company. He was lucky to have been found and was taken back into captivity; three other cubs released in similar circumstances are presumed to have died.

However, the Sea Otter Rescue and Care Program had learned from its mistakes, and when it received another orphan in June 1988, a two-week-old male called Pico, the approach was refined. When old enough, Pico was taken for supervised swims in Monterey Bay. There he was introduced to other Bay residents, including seals and sea otters, and shown how to forage for food items. As a result of these patient efforts, Pico took to his new home at Año Nuevo State Reserve eight months later like the proverbial duck to water.

Another orphan male had been reared alongside Pico. Having been found at seven weeks of age, this one—called Spock— always remained wary of humans. He became quite attached to his sibling, Pico, however. His foster mother could only hope that as Pico learned from her, so Spock would learn from watching Pico. In fact, when he came to be released, he never adapted to the wild. Both otters had been fitted with radio transmitters so their progress could be monitored, but Spock was found dead two weeks later, before the aquarium staff could intervene.

With Pico, their first rehabilitated graduate, thriving in the wild, the Rescue Team was given no fewer than seven otters in 1989. One was a juvenile female suffering from anemia and a thyroid disorder. Two little orphans rescued in May were known

Orphan sea otter with "foster parent"

as Bear and Hoppy, while another rescued male (No. 1782) remained unnamed; they were given their freedom in 1989 or 1990. Just before the juvenile female was released back into the wild in October 1989, a four-day-old male was handed in after it had been observed on its own for two and a half hours and deemed abandoned. The sixth and seventh otters were refugees from the Alaskan oil spill flown to the Monterey Aquarium for care and treatment. Orphan Annie was three weeks old when rescued; her mother was badly oiled but slipped away, no doubt to die. Kodiak was five weeks older and alone; presumably, his mother had been oiled and had already died. Neither pup was seriously oiled, nor had they ingested any oil because they were too young to groom themselves. They thrived and on August 24, 1989, were transferred to Vancouver Aquarium.

With increased experience the prospects for both long-term captive adults and newborn sea otters are improving all the time. But in the early days, because of stress, chilling and over-heating problems, even the simple transportation of otters met with an alarming lack of success. Sadly, it took more error than trial before the technique was perfected. The Russians made the initial attempts. But first, how to catch the otters? In Alaska, the Kuriles and the Commander Islands, where the animals can sometimes be found resting ashore, the otters' retreat to the sea can be cut off by researchers armed with nets. On the Aleutians,

Captive Rearing and Relocation Efforts **105**

young otters were found ashore mostly in storms. The otters slept so soundly that, when the wind was against them, they remained unaware of the biologists until they were close enough to outrun the animals. Mothers with young were the most alert and proved difficult to catch.

BRINGING THEM BACK ALIVE

Three techniques have been devised to capture sea otters alive. The first is a large landing net mounted on a pole that enables a researcher to scoop up an otter after a brief boat chase. A second method is reminiscent of the lethal gill nets used in commercial fishing—but with one important difference. The nets float at the surface, not anchored at the bottom (which has resulted in many otters drowning). Hung near otter raft sites, the floating nets are watched from a boat so that entangled otters can be retrieved quickly. This method seems to be the most effective in catching younger, inexperienced otters.

The third device is called a Wilson Trap, after the California Fish and Game researcher who perfected it. It is comprised of a net bag supported in a circular aluminium frame. The technique requires a diver to come up below a floating otter, enclose it in the net and then close off the trap with the drawstring in his hand. This trap can be quite unwieldy, so a modified version incorporates a small, torpedolike propulsion unit. The Wilson Trap is used only in waters with good visibility, so the diver can see exactly what he is doing, and a surface canopy of kelp to screen the diver's approach. The trap's beauty is that, unlike tangle nets, the diver can select the individuals he wishes to catch, avoiding, say, pregnant females or those with very young cubs.

Once an otter is enclosed in a mesh sack of a landing net or a Wilson Trap, it is not too difficult to extricate it. Held aloft by its hind legs, the creature is unable to bend its body far enough to bite its captor. The animal can also be emptied directly into a small cage, similar to the kennels used by airlines to transport pets. The captives are eventually put into floating holding pens, pending release in their new homes.

In January 1986, a team of biologists was catching sea otters for tagging off Pacific Grove, California. A large cub had just been caught, but, as it was pulled aboard, its mother circled the boat calling anxiously. She grabbed the side trying to look inside and finally hauled herself aboard to reach her cub! She too was netted for weighing (tipping the scales at 49 pounds [22 kg]) and tagging. Both were then released, happily reunited.

After an initial, frantic struggle, the otter soon settles down. In captivity sea otters quickly become tame. The Russians found that their otters thrived best on a diet of fish. Urchins were acceptable, but mussels met with little enthusiasm. The otters would bolt down seal meat but refused to touch dead birds. They ate small quantities of cooked rice and eventually sampled rye bread and dry biscuits. Americans found that fish was the most favored food, but otters would also accept octopus, urchins, crabs and clams. Starfish, canned fish and dried commercial mink food were all refused.

Sea otters have prodigious appetites, consuming over a quarter of their body weight each day. Thus, they are expensive to keep in captivity. One Seattle Zoo official good-naturedly complained that his sea otter ate more than a lion and cost more to feed than an elephant. The 1963 food bill for a single female was nearly $1,500—a male might consume a couple of hundred dollars more!

Caged otters suffer discomfort if temperatures exceed 50°F (10°C), and will die if exposed for a few hours to temperatures of 70°F (21°C). A cool air flow and dousing the fur in water helps to alleviate this discomfort. The sooner the animals can be transferred to their captive quarters the better. The Russians constructed satisfactory holding cages on the tideline, where sea water could flush and clean out the cages twice a day. In zoos, the enclosure should simulate natural conditions as much as possible. It is crucial that the animals have access to a clean pool, and if they have adequate opportunity to groom their fur, it will remain water-repellent. Should mud, food scraps or bedding get

Captive Rearing and Relocation Efforts **107**

Alaskan sea otter on ice

entangled between the hairs, however, the animal becomes waterlogged, loses body heat and dies. One rather soiled otter was released into its new artificial swimming pool and immediately sank!

If sea otters are destined for transfer to a new location, it is best to release them as soon as possible. The Russians apparently first considered translocating otters as long ago as 1907, but the first trials were not made for another thirty years. Their idea was not to reestablish otters in old, vacant haunts (a reintroduction) but to try establishing them in completely new locations (an introduction). The area they had in mind was near Murmansk, close to the Norwegian border—thousands of miles to the west of the nearest sea otter habitat. Having identified many physical and biological similarities between the Commander Islands (where the otters would be caught) and Murmansk (the new habitat), the Russians sent their nine captives on a long journey by sea to Vladivostok, but only two otters survived the stormy passage. The otters then had to endure a very long train ride, arriving in Murmansk on November 27, 1937. Surprisingly, this hardy pair not only survived their arduous trip but thrived in captivity—despite the mosquitoes, the midnight sun and cold winters, all of which were new experiences for them. In January 1940, one managed to escape and apparently survived the rigors of a wild existence for two years. The remaining captive "lived contentedly in the cage until sacrificed because of the approaching war front." This must surely have been one of the most unusual and needless casualties of the war.

 **REUNITED**

Not all stranded otter cubs need the loving care of Monterey Aquarium, however. In December 1988, two park rangers picked up a stranded cub on the beach at Point Lobos State Reserve. Beyond the surf, well out to sea, they also spotted the distressed mother searching for her cub. An inflatable boat was launched to reunite the two. The first otter that the boat reached, however, ignored the youngster when it was placed on the water, so the men moved on the next. "We approached that otter," recounted the rangers, "and put the cub overboard. The cub screamed and the mother rolled over onto her stomach and made a beeline over to it. She immediately took the cub under tow and that was the last we saw of them."

The modern scientific community would now frown upon this singular experiment. It is interesting to reflect that, had it succeeded, we would now be able to count the sea otter as a European mammal. But such aliens cause a multiplicity of problems for native fauna and flora. One need only consider the havoc wrought on the unique fauna and natural environment of Australia and New Zealand by the release of many exotic animals—for instance, stoats, deer, chamois, foxes, starlings, sparrows and rabbits. Little benefit seems to have derived from such introductions wherever they are undertaken.

 **ATOMIC AMCHITKA AND ITS OTTERS**

Although hunting pressure had reduced the sea otter numbers on Amchitka to about one hundred by 1911, the

Captive Rearing and Relocation Efforts **109**

population subsequently recovered. By 1935, it was estimated that there were no less than three thousand animals. The Japanese were suspected of poaching them, so in that year Amchitka was declared a sea otter sanctuary within the Aleutian Islands National Wildlife Refuge. Wardens were stationed there intermittently until the war intervened, during which a military base was maintained. The base became occupied in the 1960s by the U.S. Atomic Energy Commission (AEC). In 1964, it was decided to test a nuclear device—Operation Longshot—2,300 feet (700 m) underground—a scheme totally incompatible with a wildlife refuge. Biologists were permitted to monitor the effects on the wildlife, but their conclusions do not seem to be readily available.

Despite assurances that this nuclear test would be a onetime operation, another was soon on the cards. The AEC did agree to undertake some experiments to determine the shock threshold of sea otters in captivity, but none of the unfortunate animals survived. The AEC also agreed to finance the transfer of sea otters to other locations—the Pribilofs, southeast Alaska, British Columbia, Washington and Oregon. Only three new colonies were established, the Pribilofs and Oregon remaining devoid of otters to this day.

When the five-megaton Cannikin test was planned next, objections were to no avail. In 1971, the underground explosion (450 times more powerful than the Hiroshima bomb) was conducted. The AEC claimed only eighteen otters had died and called off the search for corpses within four days. Biologists picked up many more corpses, however, including seals and birds. Undoubtedly, many other corpses had been buried under rock avalanches. Although detonated 6,200 feet (1,900 m) underground, the effects of the bomb apparently drove the legs of roosting seabirds partway through their bodies. Otters resting on rocks suffered fractured skulls and ribs and internal injuries, while those in the water died from pressure effects and shockwaves. It is estimated that no fewer than one thousand sea otters could have been killed in the blast. If true, this would have represented a considerable proportion of Amchitka's otter population. Happily numbers now seem to have recovered.

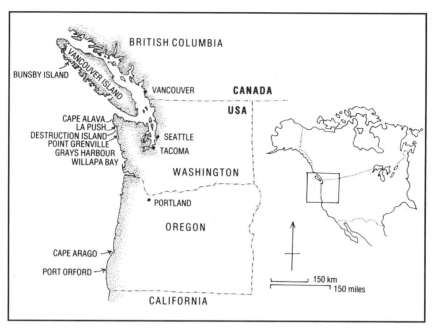

Sea otter reintroductions in British Columbia, Washington and Oregon

The Russian efforts would have been better directed toward reestablishing the sea otter in areas still left vacant following the depredations of the *promyshlenniki* more than a century before. Reintroduction was the preferred approach of the Americans. The isolated Pribilof Islands were chosen as the first venue. Unfortunately, the old problems of transporting the animals dogged the initial efforts. Thirty-five sea otters captured on Amchitka in 1951 all died before they even reached the ship that was to transport them to their new home. Thirty-one did make the journey in 1955, but only nineteen were fit enough to be released. Their soiled fur left a murky slipstream in the water as they swam away; three were recaptured by hand only minutes later, soaked to the skin, rigid with cold and near death. None of the other animals that did take to the wild was ever seen again and almost certainly did not survive. Nor did five other otters, still distinctly shabby looking, released on the island of Attu in the Aleutians the following spring. (But within a decade, sea otters

Captive Rearing and Relocation Efforts   111

had been reestablished on Attu, probably a natural colonization from the heavily populated Rat Islands to the east.)

The fur was obviously becoming soiled in transit because the unhappy otters could not groom it adequately. So it was decided to shorten the journey time by taking the otters by air. Eight departed from Amchitka on December 11, 1957. Unfortunately, a storm delayed the flight and six died that night in the overheated, unpressurized cabin. The plane had to turn back, so the two surviving males were diverted to captivity in Seattle. One died on arrival and the other survived only nine months.

In early May 1959, ten subadults were captured, but three died in the holding pen. The remaining four females and three males were flown nonstop to the Pribilofs. This time the cabin was maintained at 48°F (9°C), and the altitude did not exceed 2,300 feet (700 m). As soon as the otters displayed any signs of discomfort, water was sprinkled on their fur. They arrived in excellent condition and were liberated only twenty minutes later. They survived well in the wild, the last recorded sighting being in the spring of 1961. By that time they would hardly have been mature enough to breed, besides which seven composed too small a nucleus to result in a successful outcome. Although fifty-five more were liberated in 1968, an abnormal extension of the icepack in 1971 appears to have killed them off. And so, despite man's best but—for the otters—rather costly intentions, the Pribilof Islands, those northernmost outposts of the sea otters' range, remain untenanted.

But at least by now the initial problems in transporting sea otters had largely been overcome. In 1965, attention turned to vacant habitat farther south. Twenty-three otters were liberated on Chichagof Island in southeast Alaska. Thirty more followed the next year. In 1967, the release program received an ominous boost because Amchitka was chosen as the underground site to test U.S. nuclear weapons. The Atomic Energy Commission therefore offered to finance the translocation of large numbers of sea otters. Besides the 55 ill-fated individuals sent to the Pribilofs in 1968, no fewer than 301 others were set free at various other locations in southeast Alaska. Fifty-eight more followed the next year. In 1975, 416 adults and 65 cubs were counted from a boat;

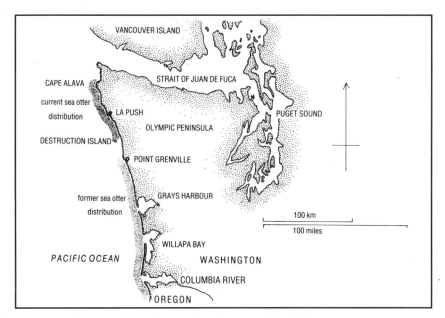

VANCOUVER ISLAND

CAPE ALAVA

STRAIT OF JUAN DE FUCA

current sea otter
distribution

LA PUSH

PUGET SOUND

OLYMPIC PENINSULA

DESTRUCTION ISLAND

POINT GRENVILLE

former sea otter
distribution

GRAYS HARBOUR

100 km

100 miles

WILLAPA BAY

PACIFIC OCEAN

WASHINGTON

COLUMBIA RIVER

OREGON

Sea otter reintroduction in Washington state

these were concentrated in a single area twenty miles from the locality where about 250 had been liberated. The southeast Alaskan population is now well established and in 1987 was estimated at four thousand animals.

Attempts were also made to return otters to the Oregon coast exactly one hundred years after they had been wiped out there. In July 1970, eighty-six sea otters were caught in Amchitka, of which twenty-four died while in captivity. Half of the remainder were destined for Washington and the others for Oregon. Two more died at Port Orford in Oregon before the holding pens were towed to the site where the otters were liberated. One returned to the port before the boat and three more by the evening. Within a week, one old female was observed at Coos Bay 50 miles (80 km) to the north, where she remained for six months. Only fourteen of Oregon's otters could be accounted for two months after their release, and three were known to have survived the winter. In June 1971, seventy-nine more were caught in Amchitka, fifteen of them dying in captivity. Forty-one were to be released near Coos

Captive Rearing and Relocation Efforts 113

Bay, Cape Arago, but bad weather hampered the operation and the otters had to be dropped directly over the side of the boat. At Port Orford, where twenty-three were to be freed, three holding pens were washed overboard in the storm. Fortunately, they burst open and all but one of the otters inside escaped. The otters' subsequent survival rate was poor, however, and about ten were picked up dead (at least one had been shot). The remainder dispersed northward along about 50 miles (80 km) of coast. In 1973, twenty-three adults could still be accounted for, but only four were noted in 1977. In all only seventeen cubs were observed, and the whole population seems to have become extinct within the decade.

Another reintroduction farther north in Washington met with more success. In historic times sea otters were common here—though probably never abundant. Early accounts mention rafts of from fifty to four hundred animals at some localities. However, by 1900 hunting had almost wiped them out, the last few being killed ten years later in Willapa Bay. On January 31, 1969, twenty-nine sea otters from Amchitka—nineteen females and ten males—were set free at Point Grenville. However, within two weeks, fourteen were washed up dead, having succumbed to stress and hypothermia brought on by their fur becoming soiled in transit from Alaska. Two more otters were shot some time later. Exactly a year later numbers improved when twenty-two more females and eight males were released a little farther north near La Push. With refined transportation and handling techniques, no deaths were reported. From this small nucleus, initial growth was slow. In 1977, fifteen otters were spotted accompanied by four cubs. Four years later thirty-six were counted, fifty-two in 1983 and sixty-five in 1985. By 1989, numbers had more than tripled from the initial release total to an estimated 211 otters. These animals range along 45 miles (72 km) of the rugged coast between Destruction Island and Cape Alava. They feed exclusively on mollusks, crabs and urchins—rarely fish, which was their staple at home in Amchitka. Their taste for urchins has resulted in an expansion of the kelp beds. The host of tourists visiting the scenic Olympic Peninsula rarely catch a glimpse of the otters, since the animals reside so far offshore and spend so much time loafing

114   Sea Otters

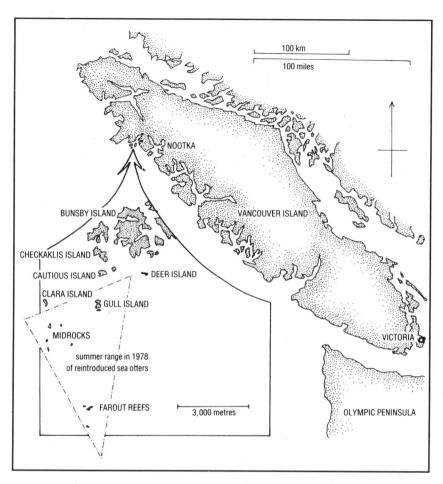

100 km

100 miles

NOOTKA

BUNSBY ISLAND

VANCOUVER ISLAND

CHECKAKLIS ISLAND

CAUTIOUS ISLAND · DEER ISLAND

CLARA ISLAND

GULL ISLAND

MIDROCKS

VICTORIA

summer range in 1978
of reintroduced sea otters

FAROUT REEFS · 3,000 metres

OLYMPIC PENINSULA

Sea otter reintroduction in British Columbia, Canada

around in the kelp beds doing very little. Food seems so abundant that they spend only 10 percent of their day feeding, and diving success is high, at around 89 percent. But such a small population of sea otters is still very vulnerable, especially to an oil spill. Nonetheless, it is hoped that they will continue to expand their range northward, eventually meeting the otters which have been reestablished on Vancouver Island in British Columbia.

The Vancouver Island population was also founded in 1969 using Amchitka otters. Twenty-nine were moved to new quarters off Bunsby Island, on the west coast of Vancouver Island. Prince William Sound, also in Alaska, provided fourteen more otters in 1970 (though many others died in transit), and a further forty-six in 1972. Other releases included thirty males (four of them cubs) and sixty females (ten immature and two cubs). Six years later, at least seventy otters were seen in the area and, although the otters had not yet increased in numbers, the prognosis looked extremely encouraging. The animals first ate urchins and then turned to a diet of butter clams. The majority of the otters occupy a triangular area of offshore reefs some 3.5 square miles (9 sq. km) in extent, where they feed and rest in the kelp beds. In 1978 two rafts were seen. One contained forty-five otters, ten of them subadults, three dependent juveniles and seven cubs, all of which must have been Canadian-born. A spring count in 1984 revealed 196 in one raft and 149 in another. By 1989, numbers had risen to no fewer than 380, and the otters were spreading out to other areas nearby.

By the end of last century, hunting had brought the sea otter to the verge of extinction in California. But a handful of elusive and resilient individuals survived in one remote location

California coast

116   Sea Otters

around Big Sur. In 1914, they probably numbered about 50 and, by the time they made headline news in 1938, there may have been as many as 300. A count in 1958 revealed 638. Ten years later they numbered 1,014. In 1969, 23 were trapped near Morro Bay in an attempt to placate local shellfishermen. Three of the otters died, but the rest were set free near Big Sur. They were all tagged, and some were later spotted back in Morro Bay. By 1976, the entire Californian sea otter population peaked at about 1,800 individuals. They had increased, albeit at a slow rate of 5 percent per annum, to occupy some 350 miles (560 km) of coastline from Año Nuevo in the north to Morro Bay in the south. This still represents only 10 percent of the southern sea otter's former range.

From 1976 to 1983, otter expansion in both range and numbers ceased, indeed reversed. Only 1,275 were counted in the spring of 1983, including some 122 cubs. The apparent decline in numbers had been precipitated by several factors. Sea otters are affected by the northward encroachment of the warm El Niño current, which often results in severe storms. Several such disasters in which otters have been picked up dead have taken place, most recently in 1982 and 1983. But by far the greatest otter mortality was incurred in gill nets—some of them one and a half miles long—set in coastal waters to catch halibut. Sea otters readily became entangled and drowned, perhaps at a rate of more than a hundred every year. Seabirds also suffered particularly heavy casualties from gill nets, so in Monterey Bay a ban was put on setting the nets in waters shallower than 10 fathoms. In May 1985, the ban was extended to 15 fathoms. However, the animals will still forage in deeper water, so the following year the ban was extended temporarily to 20 fathoms, a move that was made permanent on January 1, 1990, when Monterey Bay also became a National Marine Sanctuary. In fact, in the northern part of the Bay an emergency extension to 40 fathoms had to be imposed when more than forty porpoises were drowned in the nets. Nonetheless, it is estimated that thirty sea otters may still be drowning each year, and Friends of the Sea Otter would like a 30-fathom limit to minimize further otter mortality.

Population increase among sea otters in California is also being inhibited by illegal shooting. Both the Marine Mammal

Captive Rearing and Relocation Efforts **117**

Protection Act and the Endangered Species Act make it a crime to knowingly pursue, harass, harm, hunt, trap, capture, shoot at, wound or kill sea otters, or even attempt to do so. But, living as they do along remote stretches of shoreline, sea otters remain vulnerable to snipers who continue their wanton killing without witness. The California Department of Fish and Game is convinced that the number of dead otters found shot represents only a fraction of the total actually killed by firearms each year. In 1970, three Morro Bay divers were convicted of shooting three sea otters. The men were fined $1,000 each and given three years probation. In 1988 a twenty-nine-year-old man received six months imprisonment and a fine of $1,900 for taking a sea otter from a beach near Moss Landing; he attempted to skin it and dumped the carcass in the gutter. His girlfriend was fined $1,000 as an accessory. In 1989, one man was imprisoned for seventy-five days and fined $2,000 for driving his speedboat into an otter raft and shooting at the otters with a .22 rifle; at least one otter was killed. His two companions were also convicted and fined $3,000 and $1,500, respectively, as well as being put on probation and ordered to perform many hours of community service.

Efforts to curb otter shooting and to ban inshore gill-net fishing, together with several mild winters free from El Niño storms, have enabled the California sea otter population to regain the ground it had lost since 1976. By 1989 a total of 1,864 otters (including 290 cubs) were counted—the highest number since spring counts were initiated—with an annual increase since 1983 of 8 percent. (Not included in these totals are the 100 or more otters recently translocated to San Nicolas Island, a project to be described in more detail on page 121.) Nonetheless, sea otters are not out of the woods (or should it be kelp forests?) yet. Populations in Alaska, British Columbia and Washington have displayed annual increases between 17 and 26 percent (several times the rate in California), and scientists guess that California has a potential to support about 16,000 sea otters.

Being marine mammals, sea otters are also vulnerable to pollution. Traces of persistent toxic chemicals, filtered out and concentrated by invertebrates, can accumulate in the tissues of a predator like the sea otter. Ten carcasses from California have

118 Sea Otters

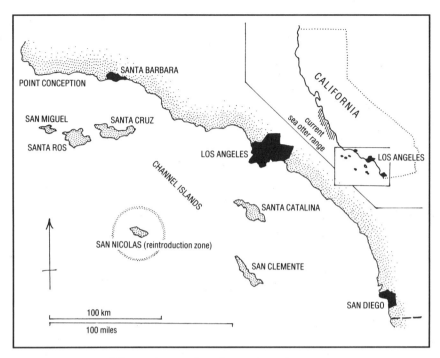

The reintroduction of sea otters
to San Nicolas, California

revealed significant levels of DDE (although the toxins had not actually caused death). Five dead otters from the same area recently were found to contain traces of Tributyl tin (TBT)—an antifouling additive in boat paint. Admittedly, these traces amounted, in the worst case, to no more than 1.2 parts per million, but such an amount is 50,000 times the concentration known to be harmful to oysters. While moves were afoot to ban this hazardous chemical from commercial and recreational craft, the U.S. Navy apparently proposed using it on its entire fleet.

But without a doubt, the most immediate pollution threat to otters is from oil. For some time, conservationists have been concerned by the vulnerability of California's sea otters to oil spills. The combined action of wind and wave could quickly disperse a slick along the entire coastline inhabited by otters. As an indication of this threat, a large quantity of timber was spilled

Captive Rearing and Relocation Efforts **119**

in the ocean off central California during the winter of 1978. Within four weeks it had been washed up on shores from San Francisco to Los Angeles. Had the cargo been crude oil and not timber, the effect on California's sea otter population—confined to this very stretch of coast—would have been cataclysmic.

Oil spills have already occurred on that rugged coastline. In January 1969, an oil well off Santa Barbara blew out, and it was ten days before it could be capped. Countless birds died horrible deaths in the huge oil slick. More recently, in 1984, a tanker broke up near San Francisco. Its cargo of 35,000 barrels of oil formed a massive and menacing slick, which, fortunately for otters if not seabirds and other marine life, drifted north rather than south. That same year another tanker, *Sealift Pacific,* almost ran aground; there was an anxious time while it drifted helplessly within a mile and a half of Big Sur, the historic heart of the sea otter's range. Fortunately, disaster was averted on that occasion. In December 1988, the tank barge *Nestucca* collided with its tug *Ocean Services* in a storm. A quarter of a million gallons of fuel oil was spilled into the sea off Gray's Harbor in Washington. Although this refined product is less polluting than crude, over 10,000 seabirds were affected, and most of them died. The slick drifted menacingly close to where sea otters have been reestablishing on the Washington coast, but only three, two of them showing signs of oiling, were picked up dead. Eventually the oil drifted north—at a rate of 12 miles (19 km) a day—to be washed up on the southern shores of Vancouver Island 175 miles (280 km) away. It is on the northwestern shores of this island, remember, that sea otters have also been reintroduced.

These incidents were all chilling reminders of the dangers to the tiny Californian sea otter population, not only from tanker traffic and from drilling operations offshore but also from potential spillages from the three oil terminals in the area. In the next few years the U.S. Department of the Interior proposes to open up 150 miles (240 km) of central Californian coastal waters to offshore oil drilling. As many as twenty platforms, each with fifty to seventy wells, could be constructed. One such could be located within 3 miles (5 km) of Año Nuevo State Reserve, with its vast colonies of sea lions (both Steller's and Californian) and the only mainland colony of northern elephant seals. At present Año Nuevo is also the northernmost extension of the sea otter's range. Otters with cubs have been seen there since 1983 (not to mention our friend Pico from the Monterey Aquarium!). To conservationists it seemed imperative to spread the otters over a wider area. The establishment of a second population of sea otters in California could act as vital insurance against catastrophic oil incidents.

Nowhere along California's Pacific coast is safe from the threat of an oil spillage, but it was decided that San Nicolas Island, one of the Channel Islands 70 miles (112 km) west of Los Angeles, offered the best venue for the new population. At first glance the forbidding shores of this bleak island, operated as a communications and missile-tracking station by the U.S. Navy, might seem an odd choice. But the wealth of its undersea resources and the lack of human disturbance should prove attractive to the otters. The project is not without its opponents, however. Suddenly, angry fishermen see San Nicolas—to this point almost totally ignored by them—as offering a significant contribution to their livelihood. They see those "gut-eating weasels" as a dire threat to the shellfish stocks. In fact, it was only after the otter reintroduction was proposed for San Nicolas that their attentions quickly turned to its resources. The U.S.Navy then had to make extra efforts to enforce its long-established offshore exclusion zone. In order to placate the fishery lobby, whose lawsuit to stop the project was successfully dismissed, the Californian authorities agreed to limit any further southward extension of the sea otter's range. Any otters found encroaching into the shellfish grounds of the Southern California Bight are trapped and removed, either back north or to San Nicolas Island itself.

Between September 1987 and March 1988, staff from California's Department of Fish and Game caught sixty-eight otters for translocation. They employed dip nets, floating tangle nets and special underwater traps operated by skin divers. The captives were then taken to Monterey Aquarium to be screened for health abnormalities. Sadly, four otters died, and another had to be released back at its original capture site. The remaining sixty-three (forty-nine females and fourteen males) were then flown by small plane to San Nicolas. Four otters were taken at a

Captive Rearing and Relocation Efforts **121**

time, each in their own individual "sky kennel." To avoid the animals overheating on the flight, all the vents had to be opened wide, forcing the poor pilot to wear extra warm clothing! Before being released the otters were first held in floating pens to acclimatize them to their new environment. Nonetheless, three males died of stress soon after release, so in subsequent years all otters were set free immediately on arrival to minimize stressful holding time.

All the animals released in the first year were fitted with colored plastic tags on a hind flipper, but these have proved difficult to distinguish in the field. One otter seen in October was not identified again until the following January. The tags have given some idea of survival and dispersal, however. By March 1988, at least eighteen of the otters were reckoned to have left San Nicolas. Eight returned to the mainland population, and one turned up in the restricted area; this female, with a cub, was caught off Los Angeles and taken back to Big Sur, where it had originally been captured. Two other females evaded capture in stormy weather, and one apparently went back to San Nicolas! (Though it is admitted that someone had probably misread a tag somewhere along the line.) Of two females found dead on the mainland coast, one had been shot; a third was drowned in fish nets and it is feared that three others may have died in a similar fashion. Out of forty-five potential survivors, twenty-four were classed as missing. That did not write them off as having died, however, for nine others classed as missing for periods of up to seven months were subsequently sighted. Only six of the missing otters were never seen again, and it is likely that some may well have lost their tags.

Only twenty-one individuals were positively sighted on San Nicolas during the seven months following their release. They grouped into two major rafts to feed on black abalones, red and purple urchins and crabs. It was unfortunate that these 1987–1988 San Nicolas otters had had to endure the worst storms on record, with 70-mile-per-hour winds tearing up the kelp beds and scattering the otters, some as far as the mainland 70 miles (112 km) away. These wandering individuals seemed to be mainly adults, so in 1988–1989 it was determined to concentrate trapping

122   Sea Otters

efforts on juveniles. By late July 1989, a further 103 otters were transported across to San Nicolas, but again only about twenty are thought to have remained. This might well be an underestimate since accurate censuses are difficult, especially when the otters are rafting so far offshore. Radio transmitters have proved useful in monitoring their fortunes. At least twenty otters have again swum back to the mainland. Ten more are assumed to have died, and fifty-five are unaccounted for, though it is hoped this will prove to be an overestimate as more individuals are recognized. It now transpires that juveniles are just as likely to wander away as adults, so in the future it is intended to select mostly mature otters. These, of course, reproduce more successfully than first-time breeders, which should enhance the project's chances of success.

Thus, although fewer than a third of the released otters seem to have remained on San Nicolas, initial results should not be dismissed as too discouraging. Other reintroductions commenced with similarly low postrelease survival, and only the Pribilof and Oregon experiments ultimately proved unsuccessful. It is intended to release a total of 250 sea otters on San Nicolas Island over a five-year period. "Previous experience underscores the fact that establishing a new otter colony is not accomplished overnight," said one official. "There are always uncertainties when you embark on a project such as this. It is a learning process, and all the knowledge gained in the first years is used to improve our operations in the future." Another scientist added, "A tremendous amount of time and intensive effort has been dedicated to ensure every possible success for this precedent-setting program, and we believe that it should be given every opportunity to succeed."

8

Threats to the Species

The immediacy of the San Nicolas reintroduction project and the dire effects of oil pollution were tragically underlined early in 1989—not in California but far to the north in Prince William Sound, Alaska. When hunting finally ceased in 1911, sea otters had been reduced to just a handful of animals in the outer southwestern reaches of the Sound, with six other remnant populations elsewhere in Alaska. Eventually sea otters were able to recover their numbers, but it is only in recent decades that they have opted to penetrate the innermost reaches of Prince William Sound. Reintroductions have aided the recolonization in southeastern Alaska, so that now the species is widespread along much of the convoluted coastline of the state. Indeed, Alaska holds 90 percent of the world's sea otter population.

Although they have been able to increase at several times the rate of their Californian cousins, the Alaskan otters have nonetheless been hindered along the way by man's activities. As we have already seen in California, sea otters can become entangled in gill nets, and the risks are no less in Alaska. In the spring of 1978, for example, ten sea otters were drowned in gill nets in Prince William Sound alone, although sixty-six others are said to have been released alive from nets. Because of its intense salmon fishery activity and recent increases in the numbers of sea otters, the Sound is one of the black spots for interactions between otter and man. Less is known of the situation elsewhere in Alaska. A survey undertaken in 1985 suggested the problems were almost as acute in several other locations—the Kodiak archipelago, the Alaskan peninsula and the Aleutian Islands. Questionnaires were returned by 143 fishermen, 30 of whom admitted to finding sea otters in their nets; 75 percent of the animals were in gill nets, 22 percent in seine nets and 2 percent in lobster pots. Between 1980 and 1984 seventy-two otters were found and only twenty-five were able to be released alive. This total represented eighteen animals affected each year, with no less than twenty-nine in 1984 alone. Twice as many adults as pups became entangled. Unfortunately, these reported deaths will represent only a fraction of the total throughout Alaska.

While the otters run a high risk of drowning, such incidents are only a nuisance to local fishermen, sometimes resulting

Threats to the Species **127**

in minor damage to their nets. Nonetheless, some otters are not being set free and instead are killed deliberately. On the first day of the 1986 netting season, five sea otters were picked up dead along a 2-mile (3 km) stretch of coastline in Prince William Sound; two had been shot and the other three clubbed to death.

Sea otters are legally protected by the 1972 Marine Mammal Act, but provision is made for Alaskan natives to kill some sea otters to make authentic articles of clothing and handicrafts for sale (providing it does not endanger the species as a whole). There would seem to have been a marked increase in this activity in recent years. Between 1983 and 1986 the number of native hunters has multiplied from three to seventy-three. Only 4 pelts were handled by registered tanneries and furriers in 1982, 31 in 1983, 74 in 1984, 385 in 1985 and no less than 555 in 1986. This total of 1,049 sea otters killed in six years is a minimum only, with no record of those poached, those not registered, nor of carcasses that were not retrieved by the hunters. Furthermore, Alaskan sea otter pelts are being smuggled to a black market in Japan, where there is what has been described as "an unquenchable appetite for frivolous articles made from the bodies of wild creatures."

The items being produced by the Alaskan natives from

Exxon Valdez *spilling oil*

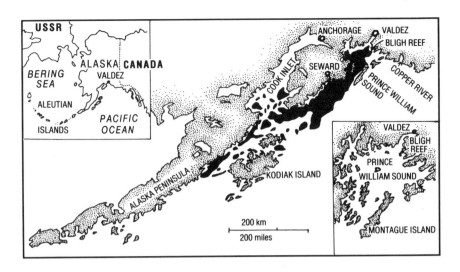

The Exxon Valdez *oil spill*
in Prince William Sound, Alaska

sea otter fur are teddy bears, pillows, powder puffs, fur flowers, etc., with only fur hats and parkas approximating "authentic" native handicrafts. In fact, because sea otters were virtually wiped out by hunting last century, and because the Russians and then the Alaskan fur companies would not allow the natives to kill sea otters for their own use, there had been no such native craft industry for nearly two hundred years. Although fully sympathizing with the efforts of the indigenous peoples to preserve their traditional way of life, conservationists see no need to create a local industry that was not there in the first place and that would open itself to widespread abuse by natives and outsiders alike.

Finally, the long-coveted fur coat of the sea otter now puts it at risk to the latest threat from the modern world—civilization's insatiable thirst for oil. Because the animal relies on air trapped in its fur for warmth and buoyancy, the sea otter is the marine mammal most likely to be adversely affected by oil spillage. Seals and cetaceans depending upon an insulative layer of subcutaneous blubber are less at risk. Contamination of more than 20 percent of a sea otter's body surface will probably condemn the creature to certain death from hypothermia, even if it avoids ingesting the poisonous chemical while attempting to groom its

Threats to the Species **129**

fur. In 1964, hundreds of tons of spilt gasoline and diesel polluted the coastline of Paramushir Island off the tip of the Kamchatka Peninsula. Russian biologists reported, "After getting into the slick, the sea otters first began to dive and turn over. Apparently due to getting wet and becoming hypothermic, the animals' movements slowed and stopped. . . . Afterward the tide carried out their corpses." It is estimated that over a hundred sea otters died. In 1988, the U.S. Marine Mammal Commission published a summary of research and management of Alaska's sea otters, in which it warned: "Possibly the greatest risk at present of an oil spill impacting sea otters in Alaska is near Port Valdez in Prince William Sound, where the trans-Alaska oil pipeline terminates. This pipeline carries two million barrels of oil a day from North Slope oil fields to the Port Valdez terminal. Seventy-five tankers per month are needed to transport this oil to refineries in other states."

Hardly had the ink dried on this important thirty-eight-page document when the inevitable happened. Near Port Valdez is a rock called Bligh Island. Curiously, Bligh had been the young master on board Cook's *Resolution* who was to gain notoriety as the unfortunate captain of *HMS Bounty* and its mutinous crew. But whatever reputation Bligh attained for posterity, he was without doubt a very fine seaman and would have been only too well aware of the danger from the reef that came to bear his name. It was a mighty vessel undreamed of by Bligh that, two hundred years later, would become the reef's most infamous casualty.

Just after midnight on Good Friday, March 24, 1989, the 30,000-ton tanker *Exxon Valdez,* 28 miles (45 km) out of Valdez with a cargo of 170,000 tons of oil, swerved to avoid ice. The captain then radioed ashore, "We've fetched up hard aground off Bligh Reef and evidently we're leaking some oil, and we're going to be here for a while"—a message that will probably prove the ecological understatement of the century.Thirty-five thousand tons (a quarter of a million barrels, or 11 million gallons) of crude oil poured into the sea. The official emergency services, financed and controlled by seven major oil companies, dithered for twelve hours. Half of their equipment was out of order. A few simple booms laid out immediately could have contained the problem.

Prince William Sound, Alaska

The company deemed this impractical because more than 200,000 barrels of oil had already escaped in the first few hours, rescue vessels in the vicinity made booming difficult and there was a risk of combustion by volatile vapors. It was to be thirty-six hours before a boom was finally laid, but by then it was too late. The calm weather, which would have made this task all the easier, finally broke. The storm compounded the problem even further by whipping the oil up into a thick emulsion, the color and consistency of chocolate mousse. The special skimmer boats found this material almost impossible to scoop up. The wind threw the oily scum onto the beaches as it pushed the slick around islands and into fjords and bays. Within a week the oil had broken out into the Gulf of Alaska, and in a month it had not only partially surrounded Kodiak Island but also penetrated up into Cook Inlet, eventually to affect 1,244 miles (2,000 km) of shoreline along the Alaskan peninsula and some 650 miles (1,000 km) from the tanker wreck. Four national wildlife refuges, a national forest and three national parks were damaged by the slick; in the case of Katmai National Park, 90 percent of its coastline showed evidence of oiling. Miraculously, the Copper River Delta, with its millions of migrant wildfowl and waders, escaped the deadly

Threats to the Species **131**

slick; so did the area's largest population of sea otters on the eastern shores of Prince William Sound.

Nonetheless, by September a total of 1,016 sea otters had been picked up dead; about 10 percent of these may have died of natural causes before the oil spill occurred. Three-quarters of the carcasses were found in Prince William Sound itself, which was reckoned to hold some 5,000 sea otters in total. No fewer than 37,000 birds of seventy-four different species were also picked up dead (only 10 percent in the Sound itself, the remainder in the Gulf of Alaska). Many more carcasses encased in the heavy crude sank without trace or were taken by scavengers. It is ironic that an oil slick on the sea can affect terrestrial creatures and penetrate so far inland. Bears and river otters were seen to come down to the foul tide—one oiled brown bear had to be shot. No fewer than 144 bald eagles were picked up dead on the shore, having become oiled as they fed on bird or otter carcasses or fish from the slick. Some 20 percent of Alaska's bald eagle population occurs in the area affected by the oil. Birds with oiled plumages, whether scavenging eagles or cliff-nesting seabirds, returned to their nests to smear the noxious cocktail on their eggs and young, with fatal consequences. Hardly any young bald eagles were reared around Prince William Sound during the 1989 breeding season; out of 339 eyries checked in the area affected by the oil, only 41 young fledged. Even black-tailed deer feeding on kelp along the beaches succumbed. Some shellfish beds have been decimated, salmon and other fisheries impacted, while many marine creatures have been contaminated by aromatic hydrocarbons from the oil. Seals were seemingly more at risk than sea lions, and although only thirty carcasses have been recovered, many pinnipeds killed by the oil are known to have sunk. Whales may have been affected too, but it is impossible to be sure. Seventeen grey whale carcasses were washed up on the beaches with oil being detected in their baleen, but such a mortality rate is little more than normal for that time of year. Thus, it is impossible to calculate the final death toll of what has been described as the greatest environmental disaster in history.

Prince William Sound is one of the world's richest fishing grounds. Encircled by wildlife refuges, national parks and forests,

Oiled sea otter

it is one of Alaska's most treasured areas of wilderness. In retrospect, many months later, there is a temptation to play down the scale of the disaster. Although 37,000 seabirds might have been picked up dead, Alaska—it is argued—is home to several millions. But scientists now agree that the actual death toll was somewhere between 100,000 and 300,000, and several local bird populations could have been wiped out, especially of some rare species such as divers and harlequin ducks. With some 5,000 or more sea otters, Prince William Sound was home to one of the healthiest populations of the species in the world. One biologist summed up their fate, "Any sea otter in the oiled area is at 100 percent risk." Only 20 percent of the *Exxon Valdez* cargo gushed from her ruptured tanks; the rest was eventually transferred to other tankers. If the captain had succeeded in his attempts to get his stricken vessel off the reef, it was possible it might have sunk, releasing a further 42 million gallons. In fact, the *Exxon Valdez* was not content with its spill in Prince William Sound; four months later, as it was being towed to a dock in California, it disgorged another much smaller quantity of oil 50 miles (80 km) off San Diego.

A thousand sea otter carcasses have been picked up—most of them almost unidentifiable lumps of black, congealed oil. Many more may never have been found. One scientist counted ninety-three sea otters on Naked Island, for instance; the next day he saw none, and no bodies were ever retrieved. Elsewhere hundreds of others were found still alive. The word *rescued* is not really applicable since even the least affected will have suffered

Threats to the Species **133**

internal complications. Inhalation of volatile compounds from the oil causes acute inflammation of the lungs. Other animals may have only slight smears on their fur but suffer hypothermia because the waterproofing and insulative integrity of their meticulously groomed coats has been damaged. Losing body heat, the otter responds by increasing its already high metabolic rate, eventually to become stressed and hypothermic. In attempting to clean off the oily mess, an otter risks a damaged gut, liver, kidneys or spleen, or else bleeds internally. It only takes some 200 parts per million of toxic hydrocarbons to accumulate in its body tissues to kill a sea otter. Even the stress of handling by sympathetic rescuers can exacerbate the symptoms. Only half of the treated otters may survive, despite the rescue centers having a staff, mostly volunteers, of two hundred.

SHAMPOO AND BLOW-DRY

The first oiled otter from Prince William Sound was brought into a makeshift rescue center in Valdez, but within a fortnight of the tanker grounding, as casualties mounted, a more permanent facility had to be constructed in a local gymnasium. These early casualties were so badly oiled that fewer than a quarter survived. Later the success rate was improved to nearly 75 percent. As the oil spread westward along the coast, a second rescue center had to be established in Seward. This center achieved a survival rate of 85 percent.

Debilitated otters had to be caught in handheld dip nets; lightly oiled, more active animals necessitated tangle nets set at the water's surface. Upon admission to a rescue center, each casualty received injections of vitamins, antibiotics and steroids, before being anesthetized for the cleaning process. Three volunteers worked on each animal, one on each side and the other at the tail, while a fourth wearing leather gloves held the jaws. The otter was first gently doused in lukewarm water, then shampooed thoroughly. Three soapings and rinsings were necessary to

Oiled sea otter being washed

ensure that all oil had been washed out, by which time the suds appeared quite white. The final rinsing had to be especially thorough to remove all traces of soap. The otter was then towel-dried before the final blow-dry, which restored the fur's natural velvety texture.

Once recovered from the anesthesia, the otter was then taken to a small wire-mesh holding cage, where it had access to a large fish box full of sea water. Here it could bathe and groom to replenish the natural oils on its coat. It enjoyed a diet of shrimp, squid, fish, scallops, mussels and clams amounting to 15 to 20 pounds (7 to 9 kg) a day. As the number of recuperating otters increased, considerable manpower was required to cut up food, give it to the otters and to monitor their progress—in addition to other mundane tasks such as washing heaps of dirty towels!

The lucky otters who do survive may have permanent internal damage, which means that they may never be able to return to the wild and are destined to live out the rest of their lives in captivity, at sealife centers and aquaria. Of those deemed to have recovered, only forty-five have been accorded their freedom—bearing radio tags to monitor their fate. Many traveled considerable distances, especially the females. Several returned to oil-affected areas, but fortunately none became contaminated again. Two otters have died. Five other individuals were dispatched to Sea World in San Diego, where their return to health could be studied closely. Although they traveled well, three died within days of arrival. Just as more of the convalescent animals were about to be sent to Vancouver, the Alaskan Fish and Wildlife Service decided to ban any further exports of live otters, claiming that adequate facilities existed in Alaska itself for the care and monitoring of oiled otters. The rescuers disagreed, but this decision seems to have been politically motivated, with local senators anxious to prove that the state can take care of its own problems.

HIGH-CLASS ACCOMMODATION

One of the first casualties of the oil slick was a one-month-old cub whose mother had been killed. The little orphan spent her first few days in a local hotel room with her human foster mother. The cub relished regular swims in the bathtub or sink, being quite dismayed when the plug was finally pulled. However, she learned to prolong her dip by diving under the fast receding water to stuff her nose into the plughole! Another favorite resort was the toilet, where she curled up so snugly into the porcelain bowl that she was almost irretrievable. Not surprisingly, she was deeply offended at being moved to the newly constructed Rescue Center, only settling down when given the luxury of her own water bed—rocked gently to sleep without ever getting wet.

Hundreds of scientists descended on the area to measure the impact of the oil on the local environment and to monitor its subsequent recovery—research that will be applicable worldwide. However, legal battles to prosecute the Exxon company and seek compensation for damage may take years. This means that many of the scientific results may have to remain under wraps, if indeed they are ever made public at all, thus totally frustrating the hard-working scientists and depriving the outside world of information which could be vital in another major oil spill. For the first time in a disaster of this magnitude, for instance, bacterial agents were tested in the cleanup and their effectiveness was closely monitored.

Only 13 percent of the spilled oil has ever been recovered, and a further 30 percent may now have evaporated; the rest remains dispersed along the shores of Alaska. Although some 60 percent of contaminated coastline now appears relatively clean, oil remains below the surface to depths of 2 feet (60 cm). Some beaches are still covered in thick mats of tar and oiled vegetation, and others are littered with rubbish left by the 10,000 people involved in the first summer's cleanup. In 1990, efforts will be scaled down, with subsequent work directed toward restoration of the shoreline. But one scientist has pessimistically concluded, "I don't think Prince William Sound will ever be the same."

With techniques in the care and rehabilitation of oil victims being improved with experience, it is imperative that oil companies learn from the *Exxon Valdez* incident; otherwise all these pathetic creatures will have died unnecessarily. The common ground shared by all concerned is that such a catastrophe should never be allowed to happen again; but the pessimists prophesy that another disaster is inevitable. Furthermore, it was almost as if the *Amoco Cadiz* and previous major tanker wrecks had never happened; nothing seems to have been learned from them. Some people despondently claim that none of the organizations involved would be able to achieve any more than they did during that fateful spring of 1989. If this, the worst of all possible scenarios, turns out to be true, surely the future of the sea otter, or indeed any other marine creature—even man himself—is bleak in the extreme. One Alaskan resident observed, "What has happened here is what I thought was never possible. People have actually killed the land."

But natural systems function on a more optimistic basis. They strive to counteract, even though the road to recovery is a slow one, and its end may never ever be reached. Mercifully—for the time being at least—the sea otter is still to be found in unaffected regions of Prince William Sound and elsewhere in

Threats to the Species   **137**

Alaska. In time the otters will endeavor to repopulate the damaged coast, just as they did when hunters almost exterminated them last century. However, the long-term effects of the oil may never permit the habitat to sustain the same high population. That is why it is vital to insure the survival of otter populations in other places, San Nicolas Island for instance. Even the otter's archrival, the shellfisherman, was prepared to sympathize with the animal in its moment of adversity. One admitted, "These little rascals get fat by eating my fish . . . but who wants to sit by and let the oil kill them off? We and the sea otters are both Alaskans, after all!" This perceptive comment is equally appropriate to the inhabitants of this whole planet, be they plant, animal or human . . . . There is only one earth and all living things are dependent upon it. Our very survival demands that we cherish it.

Sea otters ashore in Alaska

Appendix

Suggested Reading

Antrim, J.E., and L.H. Cornell. "Reproduction of the Sea Otter *Enhydra lutris* in Captivity." In *Int. Zoo. Yearbook*, 20: 76–80, 1980.

Barabash-Nikiforov, I.I., V.V. Reshetkin and N.K. Shidlovskaya. *The Sea Otter (Kalan)*, Soviet Ministron RSFSR, 1947. Transl. from Russian by Israel Prog. Sci. Transl., 1962.

Bigg, M.A., and I.B. MacAskie. "Sea otters reestablished in British Columbia." In *J. Mammal*, 59: 874–876, 1978.

Chanin, P. *The Natural History of Otters.* London: Croom Helm, 1985.

Cook, J. *Captain Cook's Voyages of Discovery*, ed. J. Barrow. London: Heron Books, nd.

Ebert, E. "A Food Habits Study of the Southern Sea Otter *Enhydra lutris nereis.*" In *California Fish and Game*, 54: 33–42, 1968.

Estes, J.A. "*Enhydra lutris*." In *Mammalian Species*, 133: 1–8. The American Society of Mammalogists, 1980.

———. "The Case of the Sea Otter." In *Problems in Management of Locally Abundant Wild Mammals*, eds. P.A. Jewell and S. Holt. New York: Academic Press, 1981.

———. "*Marine Otters and Their Environment.*" In *Ambio*, 15: 181–183, 1986.

——, and J.F. Palmisano. "Sea Otters: Their Role in Structuring Nearshore Communities." In *Science*, 185: 1058–1060, 1974.

——, N.S. Smith and J.F. Palmisano. "Sea Otter Predation and Community Organization in the Western Aleutian Islands, Alaska." In *Ecology*, 59: 822–833, 1978.

——, and G.R. VanBlaricom. "Sea Otters and Shellfisheries." In *Marine Mammals and Fisheries,* eds. J.R. Beddington, et al. London: George Allen and Unwin, 1985.

——, K.E. Underwood and M.J. Karmann. "Activity-time Budgets of Sea Otters in California." In *J. Wildl. Mgmnt.*, 50: 626–636, 1986.

Foott, J.O. "Nose Scars in Female Sea Otters." In *J. Mammal*, 51: 621–622, 1970.

Friends of the Sea Otter. *The Otter Raft*, nos. 1–42, 1969–1989.

Garshelis, D.L., and J.A. Garshelis. "Movements and Management of Sea Otters in Alaska." In *J. Wildl. Mgmnt.*, 48: 665–678, 1984.

——, —— and A.T. Kimker. "Sea Otter Time Budgets and Prey Relationships in Alaska." In *J. Wildl. Mgmnt.*, 50: 637–647, 1986.

Hall, E.R., and G.B. Schaller. "Tool-using Behavior of the California Sea Otter." In *J. Mammal*, 45: 287–298, 1964.

Harris, C.J. *Otters: A Study of Recent* Lutrinae. London: Weidenfeld and Nicolson, 1968.

Helton, D. "North to Apocalypse." In *BBC Wildlife*, 7: 376–380, 1989.

Houk, J.L., and J.J. Geibel. "Observations of Underwater Tool Use by the Sea Otter *Enhydra lutris*." In *California Fish and Game*, 60: 207–208, 1974.

Jameson, R.J., and J.L. Bodkin. "An Incidence of Twinning in the Sea Otter *Enhydra lutris.*" In *Mar. Mammal Sci.*, 2: 305–309, 1986.

———, K.W. Kenyon, A.M. Johnson and H.M. Wight. "History and Status of Translocated Sea Otter Populations in North America." In *Wildl. Soc. Bull.*, 10: 100–107, 1982.

Kenyon, K.W. "Return of the Sea Otter." In *Natl. Geog.*, 140: 520–539, 1971.

———. *The Sea Otter in the Eastern Pacific Ocean.* New York: Dover, 1975.

Loughlin, T.R. "Home Range and Territoriality of Sea Otters Near Monterey, California." In *J. Wildl. Mgmnt.*, 44: 576–582, 1980.

Mason, C.F., and S.M. Macdonald. *Otters: Ecology and Conservation.* Cambridge, England: University Press, 1986.

McCleneghan, K., and J.A. Ames. "A Unique Method of Prey Capture by the Sea Otter *Enhydra lutris.*" In *J. Mammal*, 57: 410–412, 1976.

Monterey Bay Aquarium. *Shorelines*, vol. 5, nos. 3 and 4, and press releases, 1988–1989.

Morris R., D.V. Ellis and B.P. Emerson. "The British Columbia Transplant of Sea Otters *Enhydra lutris.*" In *Biol. Cons.*, 20: 291–295, 1981.

Morrison P., M. Rosenmann and J.A. Estes. "Metabolism and Thermoregulation in the Sea Otter." In *Physiol. Zool.*, 47: 218–229, 1974.

Nickerson, R. *Sea Otters: A Natural History and Guide.* San Francisco: Chronicle Books, 1989.

North, W.J. "Sequoias of the Sea." In *Natl. Geog.*, 142: 251–269, 1972.

Ogden, A. *The California Sea Otter Trade, 1784–1848.* Berkeley: Univ. of California Press, 1941.

Pain, S. "Alaska Has Its Fill of Oil." In *New Scientist*, 123: 34–40, 1989.

Palmisano, J.F. "Sea Otter Predation: Its Role in Structuring Rocky Intertidal Communities in the Aleutian Islands, Alaska, USA." In *Acta Zool. Fenn.*, 174: 209–211, 1983.

Payne, S.F., and R.J. Jameson. "Early Behavioral Development of the Sea Otter *Enhydra lutris.*" In *J. Mammal*, 65: 527–531, 1984.

Ribic, C.A. "Autumn Movements and Home Range of Sea Otters in California." In *J. Wildl. Mgmnt.*, 46: 795–801, 1982.

Rotterman, L.M., and T. Simon-Jackson. "Sea Otter." In *Selected Marine Mammals of Alaska: Species Accounts with Research and Management Recommendations,* ed. J.W. Lentfer. Washington, D.C.: Marine Mammal Commission, 1988.

Sandergren, F.E., E.W. Chu and J.E. Vandevere. "Maternal Behavior in the California Sea Otter." In *J. Mammal*, 54: 668–679, 1973.

Scammon, C.M. *The Marine Mammals of the Northwestern Coast of North America.* New York: Dover, 1968.

Scheffer, V.B. *The Amazing Sea Otter.* New York: Scribner, 1981.

Shaw, S.B. "Chlorinated Hydrocarbon Pesticides in California Sea Otters and Harbor Seals." In *Calif. Fish and Game*, 57: 290–294, 1971.

Sherrod, S.K., J.A. Estes and C.A. White. "Depredation of Sea Otter Pups by Bald Eagles at Amchitka Island, Alaska." In *J. Mammal*, 56: 701–703, 1975.

Shimek, S.J. "The Underwater Foraging Habits of the Sea Otter *Enhydra lutris.*" *Calif. Fish and Game*, 63: 120–122, 1977.

————, and A. Monk. "Daily Activity of Sea Otter off the Monterey Peninsula, California." In *J. Wildl. Mgmnt.*, 41: 277–283, 1977.

Simenstad, C.A., J.A. Estes and K.W. Kenyon. "Aleuts, Sea Otters and Alternate Stable-state Communities." In *Science*, 200: 403–411, 1978.

Stejneger, L. *George Wilhelm Steller: The Pioneer of Alaska Natural History*. Cambridge: Harvard University Press, 1936.

Tarasoff, F.J. "Anatomical Adaptations in the River Otter, Sea Otter and Harp Seal." In *Functional Anatomy of Marine Mammals*, ed. R.J. Harrison, vol. 2, 333–359. New York: Academic Press, 1974.

VanBlaricom, G.R., and J.A. Estes. *The Community Ecology of Sea Otters*. New York: Springer-Verlag, 1987.

Van Wagenen, R.F., M.S. Foster and F. Burns. "Sea Otter Predation on Birds near Monterey, California." In *J. Mammal*, 62: 433–434, 1981.

Wayre, P. *Operation Otter*. London: Chatto & Windus, 1989.

Williams, T.D., J.A. Mattison and J.A. Ames. "Twinning in a California Sea Otter." In *J. Mammal*, 61: 575–576, 1980.

Useful Addresses

San Diego Sea World
1720 South Shores Road
San Diego, California 92109

Monterey Bay Aquarium
886 Cannery Row
Monterey, California 93940-1085

Friends of the Sea Otter
Box 221220
Carmel, California 93922

Index

146   *Sea Otters*